Tax Guide 104

RESOLVING DIVORCE ISSUES

by

Holmes F. Crouch
Tax Specialist

Published by

Allyear Tax Guides

**20484 Glen Brae Drive
Saratoga, CA 95070**

ISBN 0-944817-62-9

LCCN 2001 130376

Printed in U.S.A.

Series 100
Individuals & Families

Tax Guide 104

RESOLVING DIVORCE ISSUES

[2nd Edition]

For other titles in print, see page 224.

The author: **Holmes F. Crouch**
For more about the author, see page 221.

PREFACE

If you are a knowledge-seeking **taxpayer** looking for information, this book can be helpful to you. It is designed to be read — from cover to cover — in about eight hours. Or, it can be "skim-read" in about 30 minutes.

Either way, you are treated to **tax knowledge** . . . *beyond the ordinary*. The "beyond" is that which cannot be found in IRS publications, FedWorld on-line services, tax software programs, Internet chatrooms, or e-mail bulletins.

Taxpayers have different levels of interest in a selected subject. For this reason, this book starts with introductory fundamentals and progresses onward. You can verify the progression by chapter and section in the table of contents. In the text, "applicable law" is quoted in pertinent part. Key phrases and key tax forms are emphasized. Real-life examples are given . . . in down-to-earth style.

This book has 12 chapters. This number provides depth without cross-subject rambling. Each chapter starts with a head summary of meaningful information.

To aid in your skim-reading, informative diagrams and tables are placed strategically throughout the text. By leafing through page by page, reading the summaries and section headings, and glancing at the diagrams and tables, you can get a good handle on the matters covered.

Effort has been made to update and incorporate all of the latest tax law changes that are *significant* to the title subject. However, "beyond the ordinary" does not encompass every conceivable variant of fact and law that might give rise to protracted dispute and litigation. Consequently, if a particular statement or paragraph is crucial to your own specific case, you are urged to seek professional counseling. Otherwise, the information presented is general and is designed for a broad range of reader interests.

The Author

INTRODUCTION

Statistically, nearly one out of every two marriages ends in divorce. The divorce occurs most often between the 5th and 15th years of marriage. On average, the process of going through divorce lasts three years. During this period of time, many tax issues arise that need to be resolved. Resolving these issues — or at least pointing the way for doing so — is what this book is all about.

The going-through-divorce years are painful and heart rending. They are painful emotionally, financially, and socially. These are the more immediate pains. But an additional harm is the *tax pain* that emerges. This is a dormant pain that does not come to light until after the marital disruption process is well under way.

The tax pain borders on cruelty. For despairing spouses going their separate ways, the filing of federal Form(s) 1040 with attached schedules constitutes, in effect, a delayed punitive measure. In theory, the tax punishment is applied equally to the husband and to the wife. In reality, the punishment applies to whichever spouse federal revenue agents can locate more easily. This is particularly true where joint tax returns have been filed.

Joint returns create **unimaginable tax complications** when divorce is pending. The complications are "unimaginable" because embittered spouses take on contradictory positions which can be unreasonable. One spouse either conceals or fails to provide adequate tax accounting to the other. Misunderstandings arise simply because the process of undoing a joint (marital) return into two separate returns is much more difficult than combining two accounts into one. In the separation into "his" and "her" accounts, there are many hidden tax traps.

On tax matters of divorce, the posture of the Internal Revenue Service is fixed. Unless all facts and circumstances are clear and explicit, the IRS will take a position *against each spouse* that will produce the highest possible total tax revenue.

Because of the tax harshness in divorcing spouse situations, a "new law" has been enacted recently. This is **Section 6015** of the Internal Revenue Code. Its title is: *Relief from Joint and Several Liability on Joint Return*. Relief provisions apply where there have been understatements of tax (via errors and omissions) either wholly by one spouse, or partially by both. An "understatement," however, does not occur until one or both spouses receive from the IRS a Notice of Deficiency or a Notice of Collection Liability. At this point, the tax injured spouse may file Form 8857: *Request for Innocent Spouse Relief.* We explain the ramifications of this new law in Chapter 5 herein.

Other contentious issues between divorcing spouses pertain to child support, child custody, spousal support (before the final decree), alimony payments (after the final), and property settlement. Child support payments are nontaxable to the recipient and nondeductible by the payer. Spousal support and alimony payments are taxable to the recipient, and deductible by the payer. The result often is the intentional commingling of these payments, to the tax detriment of the recipient party. We discuss these matters with painstaking clarity in Chapters 6 and 7.

As to property settlement and the transfer of interests therewith, the process can go on for up to six years after divorce is final. This after-divorce period is termed: "Incident to Divorce." All such transfers are TAX FREE to both spouses, as per Section 1041: *Transfers of Property Between Spouses* (or former spouses). We discuss these matters fully in Chapters 8, 9, and 10. If fair property settlement is one of your pressing concerns, we urge you to read these chapters before ever seeing an attorney. Property settlement is one tax area where attorneys can really botch things up.

Divorce attorneys, as you'll find out on your own, are not very tax helpful. By training, they are preoccupied with adversarial stances in state law covering family and domestic disputes. As a result, they tend to create unnecessary federal tax problems.

Our position is that federal tax matters can, and should, be handled independently of state divorce laws. This is what we mean by "Resolving Divorce Issues." Consequently, a sincere effort is made herein to clarify the tax impacts of divorce in a methodical and authoritative manner. By doing so, it is believed that spousal attention ahead of time will spare each some of the shock and trauma . . . when the after-divorce tax ax falls.

CONTENTS

1

WARNING SIGNALS

> **Most Married Persons File Joint Income Tax Returns Automatically, Even Though Only One May Generate All Of The Income. But When Marital Disruption Gets Underway, The Returns Are Often Late Or Not Filed At All. There Are Acrimony And Suspicion, As One Spouse (Usually) Tries To Box The Other Into A Tax Corner. There Are Underwithholdings, Skipping Of Estimated Taxes, Omissions Of Income, Exaggeration Of Deductions, Interception Of Refunds, And Destruction Of Tax Notices. At All Such Times, The "Innocent Spouse" Is Kept In The Dark. Then Comes IRS Levy And Seizure: "The Last Straw."**

Marriage is a natural human relationship. So much so that it is fully recognized in tax law. This recognition is in the form of a joint income tax return. In the process, two persons — husband *and* wife — are treated as *one taxpayer*. They are two individuals, but they are only one taxpayer.

The concept of "tax oneness" of husband and wife is unique. Because of this uniqueness, undoing a joint tax return produces uncanny early warning signals of the onset of divorce. Often, the spouses themselves are not aware of this onset. It is just that the tell-tale signals in joint returning show up in many subtle ways.

When marriage is in the throes of divorce, tax disruptions occur. These disruptions become obscured by the clouds of emotion between embittered spouses. Tax complications and contrary positions grow. As a result, when divorce is finally over, one spouse — usually — is left with the burden of correcting the tax misdeeds of the other.

Divorce is a prolific source of additional revenue for the Internal Revenue Service (IRS). You will sense this on your own, as you proceed through this book. The thesis here is that if at least one spouse is aware of the tax consequences involved, he or she can take self-protective measures in advance.

Examine Your Latest 1040

If you have been married a number of years before any prospects of divorce develop, you probaby filed a joint income tax return (Form 1040) each of those years. You probably filed each year's return automatically, without reading or studying it. When there is spousal harmony, there is no real need to study Form 1040. The need arises only when spousal disharmony begins to surface.

Should you begin experiencing serious tax disharmonies, we suggest that you immediately get out your latest Federal income tax return. You should have a copy somewhere in your files. If you do not, and you know that you filed one, chances are you or your spouse has misplaced it. Or, perhaps your spouse has removed it. If this is the case, make inquiry to your spouse. You have equal right to it, if it was filed as a joint return. But don't fight over it. In Chapter 2, we'll tell you how to get a copy from the IRS.

With a copy of your latest filing at hand, take a close look at it. Look at the heading. It says—

Form 1040: *U.S. Individual Income Tax Return*

The word "individual" means either a single individual (man *or* woman), or a married individual (man *and* woman). In other words, Form 1040 applies to singles and marrieds alike. The key distinction is that the tax rates differ. Otherwise, the entries are essentially the same. A husband and wife must include all income, deductions, exemptions, and credits of both spouses on a jointly filed return.

The only way that the IRS computer knows that it is a joint return is by the checkbox being marked:

☐ *Married filing joint return*

Both spouses do not have to work (be employed) in order to file a joint return. They may file a single return jointly even though one of the spouses has neither income nor deductions. Filing a single return jointly, however, does require *two separate* social security numbers.

Only legally married persons can file a joint return That is, they must be legally married on December 31 of the taxable year for which the return is filed. The presumption is that the spouses are living together at that time. But they can live apart and still file a joint return (if legally married). By filing jointly, the income and tax benefits are shared equally. This equality applies regardless of which spouse earns the income, and regardless of whether both spouses earn income equally or unequally.

Most marrieds file joint returns for one simple reason. It is practical and convenient to do so. Where a marriage is harmonious and cooperative, there is seldom any compelling reason not to file jointly . . . and on time.

Joint 1040 Means Co-Liability

Filing a joint tax return is a privilege. It is *not* a statutory requirement. The only requirement is that "every individual" (person) who has a gross income in excess of the exempted amount shall file a return . . . and be liable for payment of tax. Thus, a married individual may file a separate return, if he (or she) wants to. There is no requirement that married persons file a joint return, just because they are married. Filing jointly is a privilege which they must elect. If they do not elect to do so, each then must file separately. There is another checkbox on Form 1040 for this purpose, namely:

☐ *Married filing separate return*

Generally, married filing separate returns produces the highest total tax on the combined spousal incomes. The total tax is reduced when filing jointly. This reduction arises because the total income is split equally between the two spouses. The effect is: twice the tax on one-half of the combined income. This way, it is irrelevant which spouse earns the higher income separately, or which has the higher separate deductions. For tax rate purposes, all entries on a joint return are "split down the middle."

There is one drawback to the privilege of filing jointly. *Either spouse can be held liable for the full tax*! The entries on the return are split down the middle, but not the tax. The full tax is enforceable upon each spouse separately This is the co-liability feature of joint returns.

This co-liability is the underlying reason for the privilege of filing jointly. Each spouse is equally liable for full payment of the tax shown. If both spouses do not pay willingly as one taxpayer, one spouse or the other will pay the full amount for both. This way, the IRS gets money no matter what the marital problems may be between the spouses. This should tell you something: taxes take priority over your marital problems.

In addition, co-liability applies to all penalties and interest associated with the joint tax. One spouse can be completely at fault for a tax misdeed, and admit so. Still, any penalties and interest associated with the at-fault spouse are fully enforceable upon the no-fault spouse. This, again, is the consequence of co-liability.

Ordinarily, co-liability for tax is no problem for married persons not contemplating divorce. But if any hint of divorce is in the offing, co-liability for current and prior joint returns filed can be — and often is — an outright disaster.

Now, Your "First Signal"

Assuming that you have your latest Form 1040 in front of you, turn to page 2 thereof. Look for the signature block near the bottom of the page. Look for the bold black print which says: *Sign Here*. See our reproduction of this in Figure 1.1. Then, read the small print above the white space for signatures. You probably have never read this before. It says—

Under penalties of perjury, I declare that I have examined this return and accompanying schedules and statements, and to the

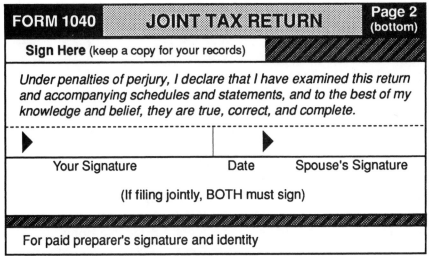

Fig. 1.1 - Contents of Signature Block on Form 1040

best of my knowledge and belief, they are true, correct, and complete.

There are two bold arrowheads immediately below this perjury statement. One arrowhead reads "Your signature," followed by "Date." The other arrowhead reads:

Spouse's signature. If a joint return, BOTH must sign.

The term "Your signature" applies to the *preparing spouse*: husband or wife, either one. Taxwise, it makes no difference. Usually, the spouse who prepares the return signs it first. The first signer also dates the return. The second signer may sign any time later. Sooner or later, both spouses must affix their own signatures before a joint return is valid.

Signing the joint return can be your first signal of potentially impending divorce. This is assuming that you are the first signer, and are the preparer (or the one who hired a preparer).

If your spouse refuses to sign your current taxable-year return, or gives you static before signing, or procrastinates in signing, you should take heed. Your spouse may be thinking things that you are not thinking.

If your spouse refuses to sign, of course you will ask "Why?". But don't expect a straight answer. Chances are, he (or she) will argue that all entries and schedules are not correct. Or, that they may not be complete. He (or she) may want time to check over the return. In all likelihood, he (or she) may suggest that you might as well go ahead and sign both signatures. Actually, this is O.K. There is always "implied consent" between spouses who are not final-divorced. Nevertheless, any form of refusal to sign should be your tip-off. Trouble may lie ahead.

Procrastination and delays are also a problem. If your spouse never seems to get around to co-signing, after you have done all of the preparatory work, you are getting strong vibes. Your spouse wants to taunt you and cause you to file late. Then, *you* will be expected to pay the penalties and interest for the late filing. He (or she) will argue that there was never any refusal to sign; you were just too impatient. This is not the kind of co-signing that goes on between harmonious spouses.

Emergence of Cunning Spouse

As you surely already know, federal income tax returns are required to be filed annually, on or before April 15. As the annual preparatory work gets underway, an interesting phenomenon emerges between uneasy spouses. They evolve into distinct tax minds. One becomes dutiful; the other becomes cunning The cunning spouse is the one who will cause the tax trouble.

The cunning spouse — it may be he or she — drags his feet and thwarts the filing deadline every step of the way. There are always excuses, and sometimes tantrums, for not addressing tax matters in a timely fashion. And, of course, the cunning spouse keeps no records. There is complaint that the government (IRS) is invading their privacy.

This does not mean that the cunning spouse is necessarily thinking of divorce at the time. He (or she) is simply trying to avoid doing his share in preparing the tax return. Subconsciously, and maybe not subconsciously, the cunning one is scheming to get the dutiful spouse in trouble with the IRS. To achieve this, the cunning spouse continually skirts and avoids all tax preparation responsibility. In many cases, the cunning spouse actually enjoys cornering the dutiful spouse into the tax hotseat.

One of the worst mistakes that a dutiful spouse can make is to not file a tax return. Yes, we know there are pain and heartache in marital dissension. We also know there is temptation to file application for extension of the tax time. This is **not** the way to go. One extension leads to another; one year blends into the next. Before long, several years have gone by and no tax returns have been filed. Records become lost. Late filing penalties and compounding interest grow and mount. The cunning spouse will blame it all on the dutiful spouse . . . every time.

In the practical world of tax preparation, there is a proven adage:

IT IS BETTER TO GET A TAX RETURN IN ON TIME THAN TO BE 100% CORRECT. ANY INACCURACIES CAN BE CORRECTED WITH SUBSEQUENT AMEND-MENTS. AVOID EXTENSIONS OF TIME.

Hence, if you are the dutiful spouse, file a tax return on time, no matter what. Whether you file jointly or separately is not the issue here. (We will instruct you how to file in later chapters.) Make up your mind to file, even if your spouse is trying to con you out of doing so.

Now you have your "second signal": being backed into a corner at the tax deadline.

Intentional Underwithholdings

A cunning spouse can deceive and tax-trap a dutiful spouse in many ways. One of the easiest is to intentionally underwithhold on income tax. This assumes that the intentional spouse is regularly employed, and that his (or her) employer is withholding federal income tax from each paycheck.

Most cunning spouses are aware of the co-liability aspects of a joint return. If not aware, they sense it, or are told about it by sympathetic friends As the prospects of divorce become more likely, the cunning spouse will begin to cut his/her withholdings.

This is done to keep more income for himself/herself and share less with the dutiful spouse.

One's first tax act upon being employed is to fill out IRS Form W-4. This form is headed: *Employee's Withholding Allowance Certificate*. Unlike a joint return, this form does *not* have to be signed by both spouses. Only the employee has to sign it. Thus, the dutiful spouse may never know what the cunning spouse has submitted to his employer.

Form W-4 permits an employed spouse to claim any number of withholding allowances that he wants. Ordinarily, a married employee with no children, no mortgage (interest) payments, and no other significant deductions, would claim "Married–2." That is, married claiming two withholding allowances. If one claimed "Married–14," for example, much less income tax would be withheld than if claiming M–2. If M–14 were indeed claimed where M–2 is otherwise proper, the other spouse would have no way of knowing. An employer is not required to notify an employee's spouse concerning entries on Form W-4.

How to Find Out

How is a dutiful spouse going to find out about under-withholding?

Frankly, there is no direct and simple answer. The fact of underwithholding may not become known until tax filing time. By then, it is too late. The dutiful spouse is stuck with paying the underwithheld tax of the cunning spouse.

If underwithholding is suspected, there is only one way of finding out before tax filing time. The dutiful spouse — somehow — must get hold of a current "pay stub" in possession of the cunning spouse. The dutiful spouse will have to develop some clever, and possibly underhanded, technique for doing so. Without the other spouse's paycheck stub, there is no way to tell. Contacting the cunning spouse's employer will do no good.

Almost all employers provide with each paycheck a stub of some sort. This stub shows the gross wages paid, the federal income tax withheld, the social security tax withheld, the state income tax withheld, and other withholdings and deductions from gross wages. The employer is required to do this for his own payroll records. So showing it on a stub requires no added effort. Besides, it is good employee relations.

If the dutiful spouse can obtain the most recent pay stub, the likelihood of underwithholding can be reliably established. The procedure is simple. Divide the amount of federal income tax (F.I.T.) withheld by amount of gross wages (G.W.). Be sure to use *gross* wages: not the net pay. Convert the quotient (F.I.T. ÷ G.W.) into a percentage figure.

Then, the following "rules of thumb" apply:

(1)   If F.I.T. ÷ G.W. is 20% or more, no underwithholding is likely.

(2)   If F.I.T. ÷ G.W. is between 10% and 20%, there could be some underwithholding.

(3)   If F.I.T. ÷ G.W. is between 5% and 10%, *under-withholding is a certainty.*

As a national average, the overall effective withholding rate is around 20% or so, for gross incomes of around $50,000. For higher incomes, it is higher; for lower incomes it is lower.

For other than exempted income amounts, the lowest *effective* federal tax rate is 10%: married, single, or otherwise. Consequently, if one spouse's withholdings are considerably less than 10%, you can be sure there is underwithholding. This is now your "third signal." The underwithholding spouse has something in mind which is not in your best tax interest.

Skipping Estimated Prepayments

An alternate form of underwithholding is the skipping of estimated tax prepayments. This applies particularly to self-employed spouses. It also applies to spouses who have sources of income not ordinarily subject to withholding. Such sources include interest and dividend income, capital gains, partnership activities, and side business ventures. All of this income is subject to the periodic prepayment of estimated taxes. A cunning spouse can easily divert attention from these taxes.

Many persons are not aware that the *prepayment* of estimated taxes is a statutory requirement. If one has sources of income not subject to withholding, he (or she) is expected to prepay 25% of the "required annual payment" in each of four separate installments. The installment dates are April 15, June 15, September 15, and January 15. If the installments are not made on time, or if the amounts are inadequate, an *underpayment penalty* applies. The penalty applies to each installment. Hence, there can be as many as four underpayment penalties each year.

A special five-page form is available for computing and paying the estimated tax. This is Form 1040-ES: *Estimated Tax for Individuals*. It contains detailed instructions, an estimation worksheet, and four payment vouchers. For familiarization purposes, an edited sample of an ES payment voucher is presented in Figure 1.2. Note that no signature is required on the ES vouchers. All the IRS wants is money: either personal check or money order (no cash). Furthermore, instructions require that the payee be: *United States Treasury*.

FORM 1040-ES	ESTIMATED TAX PAYMENT VOUCHER	Calendar Year
PAYMENTS DUE ⟶	☐ April 15 ☐ September 15 ☐ June 15 ☐ January 15	

Amount of payment $ _____ Make personal check or money order payable to the UNITED STATES TREASURY	Please type or print	Your social security number	Spouse's number
		First name and middle initial (of both spouses if joint payment)	Last name
		Address (number and street)	
		City, State, and ZIP code	

Fig. 1.2 - Edited Format of ES Prepayment Vouchers

As is evident in Figure 1.2, estimated tax prepayments can be made in one spouse's name, or in both spousal names. If both names are shown, the ES payment is presumed to be a joint payment, even if only one pays.

Estimated prepayments are mandatory when the total tax shown on a return, reduced by withholdings, is $1,000 or more. This corresponds to withholding income of around $5,000 and to self-employment income of around $3,000.

In most marriages, one spouse has more operational control over nonwithholding income than the other. If this control happens to be in the hands of the cunning spouse, the prepayments could be skipped in their entirety, or they could be grossly inadequate in time and amount. To know this or not, judicious inquiry and search by the dutiful spouse is required. If no positive evidence of ES installment payments can be found, this could be another signal that the marital disruption process is underway.

Omitting Substantial Income

Sometimes, the cunning spouse takes the lead in preparing the joint return. If significant nonwithholding income is under his (or her) control, there is an incentive for taking this lead. During preparation of the return, the preparing spouse can omit sources of income which the dutiful spouse would know nothing about.

The arrangement goes something like this. The preparing spouse gathers all information from the dutiful spouse concerning all income, employer withholdings (Forms W-2), payer reportings (Forms 1099), and estimated prepayments (Forms 1040-ES). If there are substantial sources of nonwithholding income to the preparing spouse, chances are there is no full disclosure to the nonpreparing spouse. Although the income entries are made on the proper places on the joint return, portions of the preparer's income are intentionally omitted. Nothing is said to the dutiful spouse about the omissions when getting that spouse's signature.

If the omissions of income are minor in amount, with no pattern of regularity, there is no real tax concern. Such omissions could be ordinary inadvertent oversight. About the worst that could happen would be a negligence penalty plus interest.

But if the omissions of income exceed 25% of the total income actually reported on a return, a more serious situation develops.

This amount is characterized as a *substantial omission*. Any substantial omission of income on a return brings into play a special rule (Code Sec. 6501(e)) which allows the IRS to examine all returns for the prior six years. If a substantial omission is found for three or more years, then a 75% civil fraud penalty applies (Code Sec. 6663(a)). This situation indeed becomes a serious matter.

Ordinarily, the dutiful spouse has no real knowledge of substantial omissions until, perhaps, two to three years after the fact. By then it's much too late. Corrective action cannot be taken. If the joint return shows the signature of the dutiful spouse, co-liability raises its head again.

If a dutiful spouse is suspicious of substantial omissions of income, what does he (or she) do?

The worst thing to do is to confront the preparing spouse. Suspicions are not facts. You'll never get the true facts anyway. So confrontation would only make the marital disruption worse.

When signing a joint return, the thing to do is to affix near your signature a little symbol of some sort. It can be an asterisk, a circle, a triangle, a fancy dot, or other marking known only to you. Make the symbol as inconspicuous as possible. Say nothing whatever to the preparing spouse. Your suspicions could be unfounded.

If you feel strongly about your suspicions, prepare a separate document of your own: *Innocent Spouse Declaration*. In the tax code, there is a little known section called the "innocent spouse" rule. It is found in Section 6015: *Relief from Joint and Several Liability on Joint Return*. We will not discuss this special rule now; we will do so in Chapter 5: Innocent Spouse Relief. We merely want you to be aware that the rule exists.

To help you in this awareness, we present in Figure 1.3 a sample format for an innocent spouse declaration. Our depiction is not an official form, but merely a preliminary/preparatory effort . . . just in case. You can change the wording in Figure 1.3 to fit your own case. The important point is that you prepare such declaration promptly after signing your joint tax return. Then immediately *have it notarized*! Keep the notarized declaration in your private files . . . for future need. Do this for every year that you suspect substantial omissions of income by the preparing spouse. Sooner or later, you may be assessed for the tax misdeeds of your spouse.

INNOCENT SPOUSE DECLARATION

Re: U.S. Individual Income Tax Return for Taxable Year _____ Form 1040

- -

WHEREAS on _____ , I signed (without knowing all the details) a joint tax return for the above year, I have certain reservations concerning the accuracy and completeness of the entries thereon. I have indicated my reservations at the time of signing with the symbol alongside of my name. My reservations relate to the POSSIBILITY of substantial ommissions of income and/or gross errors in deductions, over which I have no control.

WHEREAS my concerns arise solely from current marital difficulties and the prospects of divorce, I am making a protective declaration on my own behalf.

NOW THEREFORE, should it later develop that there are indeed substantial omissions and/or gross errors on my jointly signed return, I claim relief therefrom as provided by Section 6015 of the Internal Revenue Code.

IN WITNESS WHEREOF this declaration is executed this day of ___(month)___ , 20____ at _____(city & state)_____ .

_____
(your signature)
(your name typed)

- -

Acknowledgement Statement

/s/ _____
Notary Public

Fig. 1.3 - Sample Wording/Format for Innocent Spouse Record

Exaggeration of Deductions

Not all preparing/cunning spouses are in a position to omit income, even if they wanted to. If they are subject to employer withholding and/or payer reporting, there is little opportunity to omit income. But there is another area that they can pursue. They can exaggerate various expenses, adjustments, deductions, and credits that go on a joint return.

An "expense" is a subtraction from the gross income of each and every trade, business, or investment of a taxpayer. An "adjustment" is a subtraction from total income for such specific items as reimbursed business expenses, IRAs, self-employment pension plans, and alimony payments. A "deduction" is subtraction from adjusted gross income for such personal items as medical expenses, mortgage interest, or charitable contributions. A "credit" is a subtraction from the tentative tax computed for such matters as child-care credit, education tax credit, general business credit, or foreign tax credit. Collectively, all of these subtractions are umbrellaed under the general term: *deductions*. For ordinary joint returns there can be as few as 20 deduction entries. For complex returns, there can be as many as 100 or more deduction entries.

An income tax return (joint or otherwise) is actually a *summary* of specific identifiable entries. Detailed backup, with substantiating documents and information, is not required. The presumption is that most taxpayers are honest and, as humans, are subject to modest errors. A "modest error" is one which is within 10% of the true/correct/verifiable entry. A "gross error" is one which exceeds 10% or more of the correct entry.

We are not talking about modest errors here. We are talking about gross entries which are willful and deliberate. Where gross errors are involved, a *substantial understatement* penalty applies. The penalty is 20% of the amount of any underpayment of tax attributable to the gross errors.

A substantial understatement of tax occurs when the understatement *exceeds* the *greater* of: (a) 10% of the correct tax, or (b) $5,000 (Code Sec. 6662(d)).

It is a relatively easy matter for the preparing/cunning spouse to alter the deduction entries on a return, to underpay tax. There are so many places and so many opportunities to do so. It would be quite a task for a dutiful/co-signing spouse to check and verify each and every entry. To do so would provoke endless marital arguments. This risks a return not being filed at all, or not being filed on time.

As mentioned previously, the only thing that an innocent spouse can do is to affix a little symbol alongside his or her signature. Then prepare a Figure 1.3-type declaration, stressing *potential* gross errors in deductions. The declaration can be useful in the event of a tax audit, should the understatement penalty be imposed.

Intercepting Tax Refunds

Not all spouses anticipating divorce will go to the effort of deliberately omitting income, or deliberately exaggerating deductions. There is a more innocuous way to go. Simply prepare each joint return properly and intercept the refunds.

Joint return refunds are made payable to both spouses by name. This is done with the word "and" (or "&"): **not** with "or." For example, it is made payable to John A. *and* Mary B. Jones. Thus, technically, both spouses must endorse the refund check before it can be deposited or cashed. But under "tacit consent" rules, this does not stop either spouse from signing the other spouse's name. This is done all the time in marriage.

Because refund checks do not come back promptly after filing a tax return, the matter tends to drift out of attention of the non-scheming spouse. By the time the innocent spouse thinks of asking about the refund check, the intercepting spouse has long since silently laid claim to it.

One reason why interception is so easy is that the amount of refund, if any, is not boldly displayed on the tax return. Many spouses do not even know where the refund is entered. Or, if they know where the amount is shown, they do not know how to cross-check quickly its correctness. A scheming spouse could show purposely a lesser refund than actually due. This could be done intentionally to throw off the cross-checking spouse. In these situations, the IRS computer automatically pays the full correct amount of refund. The scheming spouse would know this, whereas the cooperative spouse might not.

Destroying Tax Notices

If one spouse is seriously contemplating divorce without forewarning the other, there is one "last tax signal" that he or she invariably will use. There will be vindictive destruction of all tax notices that come in the mail. The idea is to corner the innocent spouse into a *seizure chokehold* by the IRS.

In this day and age, with all the computer processing of income tax returns, taxpayers are deluged with computer notices from the IRS. Some of the notices are justified; many are not. The IRS has a whopping 35% error rate in its computer notices It pumps out these notices without any internal review or cross-checking.

Sooner or later, every taxpayer will receive one or more computer notices from the IRS. Some of the notices are arithmetic corrections; some are requests for additional information; some are denial of certain deductions claimed; some are assertions that certain income was omitted; some are demands for additional tax; some are demands for penalties and interest; some are brazen threats of seizure. And so on. Every notice carries with it the threat of loss of some taxpayer right, if the notice is ignored.

A vindictive spouse, or one who has engaged in one or more of the schemes above, can intercept these notices and destroy them. As each notice comes in, it is opened to see if it contains a refund check. If not, the notice is torn up and thrown away. The dutiful spouse is deliberately kept in the dark.

How does an innocent spouse learn of the fact that the other spouse has been systematically destroying all tax notices?

Answer: When he (or she) gets a phone call or letter advising that a **Notice of Tax Levy** has been received. The phone call or letter will *not* come from the IRS. It will come from the innocent spouse's employer, banker, stock broker, mutual fund manager, or other custodial of financial assets.

The victim spouse will be told that his or her paycheck, bank account, investment, or savings has been levied upon, and that the money has been turned over to the IRS to satisfy some tax deficiency. You will not be told by the informer, or by the IRS, what the deficiency is. This, now, is your last straw!

If you should have the misfortune of experiencing levy and seizure brought on by the misdeeds of your spouse, you really have only one choice. You bite the bullet . . . and prepare diligently for the tax trauma of divorce.

2

PREPARATORY MATTERS

Prudence Is Planning For The Worst And Hoping It Does Not Happen. If Divorce Is A Prospect, Your First Effort Is To Separate Tax Matters From Family Problems And Spousal Emotions. Gather Up 5 Years Of Prior Tax Returns And Notices. Your Marital Residence Is The "Hostage Asset" For Final Settlement. Hence, Title Deeds And Escrow Closings On Prior Residences Are Desirable. The Sequestering Of "Your Share" Of Liquid Assets And Liquid Liabilities Is Essential For Monetary Independence. When Employing An Attorney, Insist That Tax-Law Issues And Family-Law Issues Be Separated.

If the joint-tax warning signals become loud and frequent, the concerned spouse should take prompt steps to prepare for divorce. Whether actual divorce ensues or not, the preparation for it is necessary. There are two reasons.

One reason is to protect yourself from the tax misdeeds of your spouse. The second reason — equally important — is to protect yourself against the computer tyranny of the IRS. If you are the dutiful spouse, you must expect no help or guidance whatsoever from the IRS. You are their "easy target" for tax collections; they have no other interest in you, except MONEY.

Do note that we are stressing *preparation* for divorce. In no way should it be implied that we are encouraging divorce. Whether divorce proceeds to its legal conclusion (dissolution of the marriage) or not is a matter between the spouses themselves. It is not a tax matter, per se. There are tax ramifications and it is these ramifications for which we want to prepare you.

Tax Equality of Spouses

While it may not always seem so to divorcing spouses, federal policy on tax matters is straightforward. Both spouses are presumed to be co-equal. Particularly so if they file a joint return showing gross income, expenses, adjustments, deductions, exemptions, and credits. In every computational aspect they are treated as co-equal. This is so, regardless of state laws to the contrary. Federal tax laws and state family laws are entirely different. As you'll see, tax laws take priority.

The concept of co-equality of spouses is the fundamental basis upon which joint returns are recognized federally. This is spelled out in Section 6013(a): *Joint Returns* of the Internal Revenue Code. This section reads in relevant part as follows:

A husband and wife may make a single return jointly of income taxes . . . even though one of the spouses has neither gross income nor deductions.

No other body of law is so unisex as are federal tax laws. In every respect, the terms "husband" and "wife" are interchangeable. This is specifically so stated in Section 7701(a)(17): *Husband and Wife—*

Wherever appropriate to the meaning of [applicable] *sections, the term "husband" shall be read "wife" and the term "wife" shall be read "husband." Wherever appropriate* [in divorce situations] *. . . the term "husband" shall be read "former husband" and term "wife" shall be read "former wife."*

The federal tax laws take neither side in a divorce controversy. Matters of alimony, child support, property settlement, and other legal rights are primarily decisions and agreements made under state law. If these decisions become inequitable, and veer from the tax co-equality of the divorcing parties, the IRS takes a callous stance against both spouses. It will not jump on one, and be lenient toward the other. It comes down hard on both.

The IRS's position is that it is a federal tax collector. It is not an arbitrator on family law matters. It is up to the spouses — who are adults — to resolve their marital and divorce issues between themselves. If they do not, the tax ax falls inequitably on both. The result is that Big Government derives far more revenue than that to which it is entitled.

When spouses squabble among themselves, it is not uncommon for the IRS to collect the same joint tax from each spouse. Yes, the IRS can collect the same tax twice! It will do so, if the spouses are uncommunicative, and refuse to coordinate their tax affairs. This is the co-liability side of co-equality.

Never Inform on Spouse

Inevitably, as a divorce situation unfolds, one spouse begins to feel — or allege — that the other is getting the better tax break, or is getting away with something. To the spouse feeling this way, the premise of tax equality is a hoax. This provokes a desire to "right the scales" of justice by informing on the other spouse to the IRS. The informing spouse then expects the IRS to punish the accused spouse. Punishing a spouse is not what the tax laws are about.

Informing on one's spouse to the IRS is a horrible mistake. In the first place, the IRS is not the least bit interested in achieving tax justice between disputing spouses. Secondly, because the informing spouse is so unknowledgeable in tax administration, issues are raised that were never intended to be raised. A whole new can of tax worms can be opened up. Informing not only calls attention to the spousal returns, past and present, but also calls attention to the returns of persons associated with the spouses.

When a spouse reports any alleged tax misdoing, the IRS will computer-in on everything it possibly can, to collect maximum revenue. More often than not, the situation backfires totally against the informing spouse. The following is a real-life case example.

The husband was in a small business with a male partner who was flaky on matters of tax accounting. The partner kept all the books and prepared the tax return information. The husband reported his share of the partnership income, deductions, and credits on the joint tax return with his wife (the informant). The wife thought that the husband was getting away with something. She threatened to report him to the IRS unless he came clean to her. The husband's conscience was clear. He said to his wife: "Go ahead and report me." She did. She proceeded to make an in-person report/complaint to the local IRS office: Informants Examiner.

Guess what happened?

The IRS went through its routine computer search procedures. It found that there was an outstanding tax deficiency by the husband's partner (and the partner's wife) in the amount of $28,630. With penalties and interest, the cumulative assessment against the husband's partner was $51,910. The partner and his wife had just gone through divorce, and the IRS could not find them. The IRS then demanded full payment of the $51,910 from the informing wife and her informed-upon husband!

The husband was angered and incensed by this. He did nothing wrong. The partner did: not he. In this case, the husband claimed the innocent spouse rule and made it stick. The assets of the informing spouse were then levied for the full $51,910 . . . plus additional penalties and interest.

This levying against the informant comes under the tax-legal theory of *joint and several liability*. Anyone associated (in a business relationship) with a delinquent taxpayer can be held liable for the entire delinquency.

The moral above is obvious. One spouse should never inform on the other spouse to the IRS. The informing spouse only helps the IRS and makes matters much worse between the spouses themselves.

Gather Prior Tax Returns

Many married persons are downright careless about keeping copies of their joint tax returns. To many, filing an income tax return is a once-a-year crisis. They delay it as long as they can. They panic as they rush to get it filed on time. When the crisis passes, they toss aside their copy, hoping never again to have to look at it.

If the marriage is harmonious, and the couple pays maximum taxes each year, and they are absolutely sure of the correctness of entries, no real harm is done in not keeping copies of their returns.

But the moment the hint of divorce is in the air, the prior returns suddenly become very important documents. There is a lot of vital information on a tax return which you cannot remember from year to year. (Skim read Figure 2.1 to see what we mean.) Usually, prior returns are nowhere to be found. If any are available, it is probably only the most recent one. One tax return is not enough of a record. If one is preparing for divorce — albeit reluctantly — he (or she) is advised to gather together at least **five years** of returns. If you have been married less than five years, gather all that you have filed. If you have been married more than five years, the last five are sufficient. Rarely are more than five years of returns needed.

What if you don't have five years of tax returns around the house? For a small fee, you can request copies from the IRS.

There is a special form for this, namely — **Form 4506**: *Request for Copy or Transcript of Tax Form.* Instructions on the back of the form tell you where to mail your request. The instructions on the face of the form allow you to request up to four years of tax returns. You will have to prepay $23.00 for each tax period requested. Allow three to six months for delivery.

On the face of Form 4506, there are the usual spaces for name(s), address, social security number(s), tax year(s), and so on. You are then instructed—

Check the box to show what you want:
☐ *Copy of tax form and all attachments.*
☐ *Certified copy for court or administrative proceedings.*
☐ *Copy of Form(s) W-2 only* [No charge].

The beauty of Form 4506 is that it requires *only one signature.* Each spouse can make a separate request for prior returns, provided the requester's name and signature are on the joint return for the year requested. Thus, it is inexcusable for either spouse contemplating divorce not to have a five-year set of tax returns. It takes at least five years of returns to establish any pattern of "tax tinkering" by the other spouse.

RESOLVING DIVORCE ISSUES

NAME(S), ADDRESS, OCCUPATION(S), SOCIAL SECURITY NUMBER(S)
1. FILING STATUS Joint, Separate, Head of Household, Single
2. EXEMPTIONS Yourself, Spouse, Children, Parents, Others
3. SOURCE OF INCOME • Wages, Salaries, Tips, Bonuses • Supplemental Gains or Losses • Interest & Dividend Income • Pension, Annuities, IRA Distributions • Business Income or Loss • Rents, Royalties, Estates, Trusts • Capital Gain or Loss • Farm Income or Loss
4. ADJUSTMENTS TO INCOME • Job Related Moving Expenses • Deductible IRA's & SEP's • Self-Employment Pension Plans • Alimony Payments
5. SCHEDULES ATTACHED A. Itemized Personal Deductions B. Itemized Interest & Dividends C. Business Income & Expenses D. Capital Gains & Loss E. Supplemental Income Sources F. Farm Income & Expenses
6. TAX COMPUTATION Standard, Itemized, Capital Gains, Kiddie Tax, Other
7. NONREFUNDABLE CREDITS Dependent Care, Child Credit, Educational Tax Credit(s), Special Business Credits, Prior Year Minimum Tax Credit
8. OTHER TAXES Self-Employment, Alternative Minimum, Recapture Taxes, Tip Tax, Premature IRA and Pension Withdrawals
9. PAYMENTS MADE Withholdings, Estimated Prepayments, Extension Payments, Excess Social Security Tax, Refundable Credits
REFUND OR AMOUNT OWED

Fig. 2.1 - Outline of Vital Information on Form 1040

Gather Tax Notices & Records

As you get your tax returns together, also search diligently for any tax notices and any records that back up the entries on those returns. Go through all of your files and papers around the house, and get them organized. If it will not cause a major blowup, ask your spouse to help you. You are not trying to get anything on your spouse. You simply want to avoid any tax surprises down the line.

Organize the IRS notices and your records by **tax year**: *not* their posting dates. Put each year's papers in a large envelope or folder. Make a separate file for each year and properly mark it. Tell your spouse that these records are available for his (or her) use also. If your spouse knows that you are updating and organizing the joint tax records, there is less likelihood of wild allegations being made against you.

If you are uneasy about your spouse and wonder whether any IRS notices have come through that you do not know about, phone or visit your local IRS office. Give the IRS both of your social security numbers. Tell them that you recall receiving some notice from them but, somehow, you have misplaced it. You want to find out what it was, so that you can respond. Ask them to check their computer and see if anything is outstanding in your account.

When you make inquiry to the IRS, do not reveal any of your marital problems. Do not even hint at them. Play it cool.

If there is any unfinished business with the IRS, tackle it and try to resolve it. It is cheaper to clean up any tax problems now rather than after the divorce. If your spouse will not cooperate, the matter becomes an issue to settle in the divorce proceedings.

"What Can Happen" Example

Divorce situations are prolific sources of additional tax revenue. When spouses are noncooperative and contradictory, the IRS makes out . . . most every time. This is a sad commentary on our tax system. New law, as presented in Chapter 5, eases the situation somewhat.

Let us cite, now, a true case. Levy ensued as a direct result of the bickering and noncommunication between spouses. They had a marital residence on which they were making mortgage payments, and they had income property which they rented to another family.

The bickering couple had been married 12 years and had two children. Marital quarrels grew worse and worse. One evening, the husband assaulted and battered his wife. She called in the police, who evicted him from their home. Thereupon, the wife went to an attorney to start divorce proceedings He instructed her never to allow the husband in the house again, and to cease all communications with him (including phone and mail). The wife construed this as her legal weapon for punishing her husband.

Shortly afterwards, the wife received an envelope from the IRS addressed to both spouses. They had filed joint returns throughout their 12-year marriage. Because the envelope was from the IRS, the wife saw a chance to get even with her husband. She threw away the envelope and its contents, without opening it.

For the next several months, she received other envelopes from the IRS. As each one arrived, she threw it away. The wife was not working at the time, though she had previously worked intermittently, part time. The husband was fully employed.

The first inkling that the husband ever had of the IRS communication was from his employer. He was called into his manager's office one day and handed a copy of NOTICE OF LEVY. It was accompanied by an IRS demand for $5,555 (actual figures). There was no explanation whatsoever.

The husband immediately went to the nearest IRS office with the levy in hand. He wanted an explanation. He was told to contact the regional processing center at Fresno, California. He phoned there. After being routed among several taxpayer assistance desks, he was told: "We will send this information to you. What is your present address?"

The following week he received Form 1902-B: *Report of Individual Income Tax Examination Changes*. The report showed—Year: 1991; Form: 1040; Filing Status: Joint. It was accompanied by a handwritten explanation that—

Since you did not answer our previous letter requesting supporting information, we have disallowed all of the deduction amounts that you claimed.

The amounts claimed were readjusted as follows:

	Amount Claimed	Amount Allowed	Adjustment Increase
Interest expense	$3,362	-0-	$ 3,362
Misc. deductions	1,146	-0-	1,146
Medical expenses	258	-0-	258
Rental interest	4,642	-0-	4,642
Rental taxes	1,407	-0-	1,407
Rental utilities	465	-0-	465
Rental expenses	3,137	-0-	3,137
Rental depreciation	2,099	-0-	2,099
	Total adjustment increase		$13,317
	Tax increase		4,211
	Penalties & interest		1,344
	Total demand		$ 5,555

Protest When Right

The husband contacted Fresno IRS again by phone. He was told to write a (protest) letter explaining his position on the matter. Six months later he received an answer—

You must pay the tax due, if you want your case to be given further consideration.

By this time the demand amount had grown to $7,047 due to added penalties and interest. Fortunately, the husband had kept good records and knew that the IRS was dead wrong.

The husband did not pay the $7,047. Instead, he complained against the IRS to his Congressman. Subsequently (in May 1994), through the efforts of his Congressman, an audit appointment was arranged at the local IRS office. The husband sent his tax preparer to the audit.

The results of the audit?

The revised Form 1902-B read—

Tax as previously adjusted	$7,047
Overassessment (decrease in tax)	(4,211)
Correct tax	2,836
Abatement	4,211
Penalty	-0-
Interest	-0-

The "correct tax" was exactly the same figure ($2,836) shown on the original return. There was no net audit change whatsoever!

The original inquiry that the IRS sent to the joint taxpayers pertained to an *illegible* W-2 for the wife, submitted with the original return. The wife should have responded; not the husband. Yet, she put him through three years of anxiety, and subjected his wages to a $7,000[+] IRS seizure.

The blame in this case lies largely with the wife's attorney. Instead of being so adamant, he should have used his head. He should have instructed the wife to open all letters, notices, and statements from tax authorities, review them, and, if applicable, send them on to the husband. She certainly knew his address; that's where the Sheriff served him her Petition for Divorce. The attorney also knew the husband's address; that's where he billed for collection of his fee.

Deeds & Escrow Papers

Much of the preparatory effort that we are discussing is just plain updating of personal records. Married couples preoccupied with everyday matters of family living tend to get lax on record-keeping. An occasional spur is needed to overcome the pattern of laxity. Preparation for divorce can provide this spur, even if divorce never becomes reality.

The most important property asset in marriage is the family residence. It is the one item which is used to balance all issues, pay off all debts, and make a final, equitable settlement between the spouses. It is the primary negotiating asset in divorce proceedings, and, as such, it is held hostage to the bitter end. For this reason, it is often referred to as the *hostage asset* of marriage.

It is tragic how important papers on this hostage asset get lost, misplaced, or unrecognized. Important, too, are the papers on all prior residences of the married couple. There are ownership trails to be retraced; and there are tax trails to be fixed. If the spouses did not contribute equally to the cash down on purchases, this fact could become a bargaining item when the current marital residence is partitioned.

What residence papers do you need?

You need the latest recorded *title deed* to your current residence. This may be a grant deed, a trust deed, a joint tenancy deed, a community property deed, or other official document with the word "deed" on it. A deed designates the owner(s) of the property and gives a legal description of it. Encumbrances and covenants thereon may also be indicated. Not everyone knows what a deed looks like. If you are one of these persons, a glance at Figure 2.2 may be helpful to you.

You need the *settlement statement* on the purchase of your current residence. This statement is prepared by an escrow officer, a title company, or a real estate attorney. This statement summarizes all financial particulars of the transaction: purchase price (or selling price), cash down, mortgage obligation(s), commissions, closing costs, property taxes, creditor liens, local assessments, and other matters. You want the final statement only: not the tons of preliminary papers leading up to the final closing. The closing statements on prior residences can be helpful when spouses contribute unequally to the purchase price.

You need any and all *loan application(s)* for mortgages and other borrowed money on your current residence. This includes all improvement loans, pool (and roof) loans, equity loans, and refinancing of your residence. These applications reveal vital information on your financial status (your assets and liabilities), which you may have forgotten. Also, get loan statements on the balance outstanding at the end of the last calendar year. This way, you will know the total encumbrances on your home. Ideally, you would like to establish the amount of *equity* (value minus debt) in your home. Equity is the amount of potential cash available, should the necessity arise that the home be sold. Here is the "cash pool" for finalizing all aspects of a divorce.

Upon Recording Mail to:	Instrument No._____
_____	Book _____ , Page _____
Donald C. Buyer	Date Recorded _____
Jane D. Buyer	OFFICIAL RECORDS
(address)	County of _____

GRANT DEED

For valuable consideration, receipt of which is hereby acknowledged

JOHN A. SELLER and MARY B. SELLER,
husband and wife

HEREBY GRANT TO -

DONALD C. BUYER and JANE D. BUYER,
husband and wife, as joint tenants with right
of survivorship

ALL THAT REAL PROPERTY situated in the city of _____ ,
County of _____ , State of _____ , described as
follows to wit:

(Full legal description of
property transferred)

IN WITNESS WHEREOF this instrument is executed this
day of _____ , 20_____ .

Verification
and Seal of
Notary Public

/s/_____
John A. Seller

/s/_____
Mary B. Seller

Fig. 2.2 - General Format of Deed: Marital Residence

Sequester "Your Share" Only

Be under no illusion. Divorce is costly in time, emotion, and money. Mostly money. You will need adequate money in reserve, and it is best that it be under your sole control. So here, too, preparatory effort is required.

As unobtrusively as you can, start sequestering (corralling) your share of the marital liquid assets. A "liquid asset" is money in checking/savings accounts, certificates of deposit, mutual funds, marketable securities, brokerage accounts, credit cards, and so on. You want to record and sequester these assets carefully and quietly. You don't want to raise suspicion or cause uneasiness to your spouse. Nor do you want to take advantage of your spouse. All you want to do is set aside *your share* of the marital estate.

For example, suppose you have a joint savings account with a balance of $15,269 on the day you decide to start sequestering. Your first step is to photocopy the information when the account was first opened, and that information showing on the current date. If you were married when the account was opened, and all deposits then and thereafter were made from marital funds, your share would be 50% or $7,634. Withdraw no more than this amount. Place it in a separate account, in a separate institution, in your own name. Don't try to one-upmanship your spouse.

The same principle of sequestering applies to mutual funds, brokerage accounts, and other investment sources. If you contributed money to any of those accounts from nonmarital funds, you are entitled to full recovery of the nonmarital money. Nonmarital money is that which you had before marriage, and that which you received during marriage by gift or inheritance. You must be able to convincingly trace all alleged nonmarital funds.

On the other side of the coin, if your spouse contributed nonmarital funds to any of your joint accounts, you are not entitled (for sequestering purposes) to any of those funds. It takes a person who is mature and confident not to overstep into the proper share of your spouse. The sharing may be quite different at a time of final divorce. But right now, we are only concerned with sequestering your own money, and 50% of marital money, in order that you can weather the divorce proceedings financially independent. To provide you some guidance in this regard, we present Figure 2.3.

The important point to be aware of is that sequestering is *not* a marital property settlement. Such is a matter for the divorce court to establish later. As indicated in Figure 2.3, sequestering focuses solely on liquid assets and liquid liabilities (credit cards). The sole purpose being sought is monetary independence from your spouse.

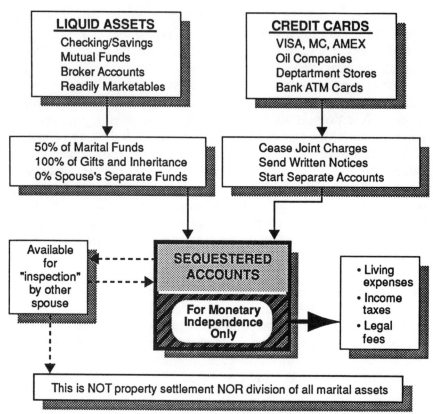

Fig. 2.3 - Sequestering "Your Share" for Monetary Independence

The primary liquid liability of a marriage is the widespread use of credit cards and charge accounts. If you have multiple cards with husband and wife duplicates, you have a problem. Your solution is to cut down on all credit charges and save your money. This sounds simple enough. But how do you do this without confronting your spouse who may be charging up a storm?

There is only one practical solution. You cease all charges against joint credit card accounts. Do this, then notify all card issuers that, after a designated date, you will not be liable for any charges. Set up separate checking, savings, and charge accounts in your own name, and pay your own bills.

The misuse of money and credit cards is often the explosive force which finally drives many married persons to divorce. A good sequestering plan, therefore, is essential to the preparing spouse's financial survival.

Necessary Legal Proceedings

Marriages may be made in heaven, but divorces are made in court. The "court" is that which has legal jurisdiction over all persons within its political boundaries. In most states, this is the Superior Court of the county where one or the other of the spouses resides (with a valid address).

In every case of legal marriage, there has to be some kind of dismarriage proceeding. The proceeding takes time; it requires the filing of certain papers and paying certain costs. The time, papers, and cost vary for each state. The end result is a Final Judgment: Dissolution of Marriage whereby—

The parties are restored to the status of unmarried persons.

Until a final legal decree is obtained, the parties are married even though they may live apart, maintain themselves separately, and take joint, mixed, or separate custody of the children.

Under regular dissolution procedures, most states require as a minimum three legal steps, namely:

1. Petition for Dissolution
2. Interlocutory Order
3. Final Judgment

A Petition is necessary to set the legal process in motion. The spouse initiating the divorce proceedings is called the *petitioner*; the other spouse is called the *respondent* (whether he/she responds or not). The court for jurisdiction is in that state where the petitioner has resided for at least six months (typically) and in that county where he/she has resided at least three months (typically). The Petition states the date and place of marriage, the date of separation, the names and ages of children, and the social security numbers of both spouses. The applicable statutory grounds for divorce also are indicated.

The Petition has to be served upon the respondent by a party other than the petitioner himself/herself. This can be any third party. More often than not, service is made by a member of the County Sheriff's Office. The responding spouse is allowed 30 days (typically) to answer. The "answer" may be affirmative, negative, or nonresponsive; it may be a responsive declaration or a cross-petition. The nature of the answer pretty well establishes whether the proceedings will be amicable and expeditious, or fierce and drawn out.

The Interlocutory Order is a temporary judicial decree. It requires the presence of at least one of the spouses in court. At the hearing (trial), opposing attorneys try to thrash out the spousal differences on particular state-law issues. These issues pertain to child custody, child support, parental visitations, spousal support, description of marital property, statement of marital debts, restraining orders, and tentative property settlement terms. Upon conclusion of the trial, the judge signs an Order.

The Interlocutory Order is a procedure for forcing spouses to come to some preliminary agreement on family matters of interest to the state of domicile of the petitioner. It has little or no significance for federal tax purposes.

The Final Judgment is a restatement of the interlocutory terms where there has been no change; a revision/clarification of child support amounts; the setting of alimony terms; and distribution of the assets and liabilities of the marital estate. If so requested by the wife, she can have her former name restored.

The three procedures above are the minimum necessary to get a divorce in most states. These procedures are summarized in Figure 2.4. Each is evidenced by a separate legal document of its own. The time between filing a petition and getting a final decree varies from state to state: six months to three years (or longer). The longer the proceedings, the greater the legal fees.

Precautions with Attorneys

At some point in time, you will need an attorney to pursue the legal proceedings above. But we urge you not to go to an attorney until you are fully prepared. We also urge you not to go until after

Name, address, phone number of Attorney(s)	Space for Court Clerk
Re: The Marriage of: Petitioner: _____ Respondent: _____	IN THE SUPERIOR COURT STATE OF _____ COUNTY OF _____ CASE NO. _____

① ➡ PETITION FOR DIVORCE

- Residency requirements
- Date & place of marriage
- Date of separation
- Name(s) & age(s) of children
- Statutory grounds

② ➡ INTERLOCUTORY ORDER

- Date respondent served
- Uncontested or contested
- Which spouse present
- Custody and care of children
- Spousal support needs
- Full disclosure of property
- Debt obligations assigned
- Likely property settlement

③ ➡ FINAL DECREE

- Statutory waiting period
- Revision of interlocutory
- Child support terms
- Alimony payments
- Property settlement

Fig. 2.4 - Minimum Legal Procedures for Divorce

you have read this book. You need to know ahead of time what you are getting into.

It is a grave mistake to rush off to an attorney at the first inkling of divorce. It is a mistake because, by profession, attorneys are not problem solvers: they are problem creators. They often make matters worse. They tend to "point and counterpoint" over theoretical legalities which obscure the real issues. They tend to deliberately drag out matters, rather than settling them expeditiously. The "deeper the pockets" of a client, the longer they delay. However, although you might like to, you cannot do without them.

Thus, when you do go to an attorney, we offer the following precautions:

Caution 1. Do not employ an attorney to do things which you can do for yourself. You are more knowledgeable in your own affairs, and more interested, too. This means doing your homework all along the way. This also means be prepared with facts, figures, dates, and documents.

Caution 2. Interview two or three different attorneys before you commit to one. One-half hour or so with each is all you need. You want to establish whether there are any communication, cooperation, or "chemistry" barriers between yourself and the attorney. Touch only on the highlights of your case, to see if the attorney is interested.

Caution 3. Be leery about retainer fees. Some attorneys treat retainers as a pure bonus for the privilege of taking on your case. Others treat the retainer as a fee advance, to be applied against your bill at an hourly rate. A retainer is to cover upfront time in case you change your mind. It is seldom refundable.

Caution 4. Do not rely on an attorney to instruct or educate you on the applicable law(s) in your case. Attorneys tend to paraphrase a law in a manner designed to intimidate you against further inquiries. Rarely will an attorney quote a specific law, as we have done (and will do) herein.

Caution 5. Very few divorce attorneys are expert in tax matters. They know the basics, but not the detailed tax forms and computer printouts that emanate from the IRS. Most of the tax haggling goes on long after a divorce is finalized. So, don't rely too heavily on attorneys for tax advice. Seek on your own a tax professional who has relevant experience.

Separation of Tax Issues

The time between filing a petition for divorce and obtaining a final decree is plagued with tax uncertainties. These uncertainties occur because this time span is a vast grey area of tax law. It is a grey which is muddied and confused by the volume of "legal papers" prepared, filed, and stipulated by attorneys. Most attorneys lack the training and self-discipline to sort out tax from nontax matters. The sorting out *can be done*, if so insisted on.

Our recommendation here is for each spouse to take it upon himself (herself) to insist that his attorney separate out all tax matters. The key to doing so is to organize the tax issues into specific subjects, then prepare a separate, self-explanatory statement/ document on each subject. The statement on each tax subject need be only one clear paragraph, or one page at most. Each tax issue can be annexed to the applicable legal document without jeopardizing the adversary position of either spouse under state law. The separation of tax matters from family matters becomes an excellent preparatory tool for winning an IRS audit, several years down the road.

What are the tax issues (subjects) to be separated? There are six. We will discuss each in depth in subsequent chapters of this book.

In the meantime, though, let us identify the six subjects by the capital letters A, B, C, and so on. In this way, each can be annexed as Exhibit "A", Exhibit "B", etc. to its related legal document.

The six tax subjects are—

"A" — Separate Maintenance Order
"B" — Child Support Order
"C" — Disclosure of Marital Property
"D" — Alimony Payments
"E" — Property Settlement
"F" — Disposition of Marital Residence

How these tax subjects relate to the basic legal steps is shown in Figure 2.5. Each tax subject can piggyback the legal process in each state, yet be separable from that process for subsequent tax analysis and determination. There is no reason for divorcing spouses to be kept in the dark on tax matters.

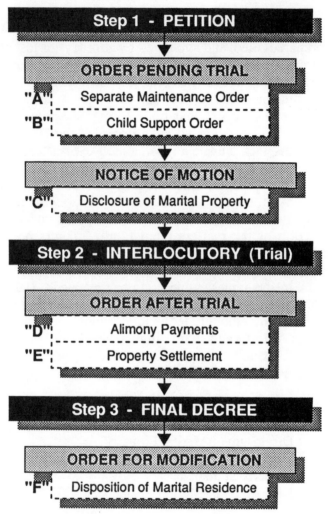

Fig. 2.5 - Sequence of Separation/Annexing of Tax Matters

3

MARITAL STATUS

One's Marital Status For Tax Purposes Is Determined As Of December 31 Of Each Year. Under Certain Conditions, Married Persons In Process Of Divorce (Who Are U.S. Citizens) May Be "Deemed Unmarried." If So Deemed, Each Spouse May File A Separate Return As A Single Person Or As Head Of Household. This Can Substantially Reduce Their Total Tax. Otherwise, They Must File Married Jointly Or Married Separately. A Married Separate Return Can Be Filed With Or Without The Knowledge Or Consent Of The Other Spouse. This Often Produces A Higher Total Tax, But Other Than Tax Considerations May Prevail.

The marriage process is a matter for state law. So, too, is the divorce process. Neither marriage nor divorce comes under the province of federal law. This is because marriage and divorce (and remarriage) are deemed to be strictly domestic affairs under the family laws of the state of domicile. Unfortunately, state family laws distract spouses from knowing their proper marital status for federal tax purposes. The longer the divorce proceedings, the greater the agony of uncertainty in federal tax filings.

In this chapter we want to discuss (in some detail) the federal treatment of marital status. Ordinarily, if a couple is legally married, he and she remain legally married, until the marriage is legally dissolved. But, as you will see below, married persons undergoing divorce have several options that they can pursue for federal income tax purposes. These federal tax options, however, do not alter the status of marriage in their state of legal residence. The federal purpose is to encourage the filing of tax returns on time.

Tax Code Section 7703

Section 7703 of the Internal Revenue Code specifically addresses the period between petition for divorce and the final decree. It recognizes the tax predicament of spouses going through an extended dissolution process. Thus, for tax purposes, it is immaterial how long this process takes: 1, 3, 5 years or whatever. Section 7703 is designed to circumvent the conflict of state divorce laws with federal tax laws, and to provide a consistent basis nation-wide for filing proper tax returns.

The official title of Section 7703 is: *Determination of Marital Status.* It consists of two subsections, namely: (a) general rule, and (b) special "living apart" rule. Section 7703 is a very important tax law for spouses undergoing divorce. It substance should be memorized.

In pertinent part, Section 7703 reads as follows:

(a) *General rule*

(1) The determination of whether an individual is married shall be made as of the close of his taxable year;
(2) An individual legally separated from his spouse under a decree of divorce or of separate maintenance shall not be considered as married.

(b) *Certain married individuals living apart*

*(1) If an individual who is married (within the meaning of subsection (a)) and who files a separate return maintains as his home a household which constitutes for more than one-half of the taxable year **the principal place of abode of a child** . . . with respect to whom such individual is entitled to a deduction [exemption] for the taxable year (or would be so entitled), . . . and*

(2) such individual furnishes over half the cost of maintaining such household during the taxable year, and (3) during the last 6 months of the taxable year, such individual's spouse is not a member of such household, [then] . . . *such individual shall not be considered as married.* [Emphasis added.]

Section 7703 is not a substitute for legal proceedings in divorce. It merely establishes guidelines for filing federal tax returns as unmarried persons. Many state tax laws also follow Section 7703 during the divorcing period.

The statutory characteristics of interest to us are as follows:

One. Tax filing status is determined at the end of each year: on or before midnight December 31. Thus, spouses can alter their filing status by advancing or postponing their actions relative to December 31.

Two. Prior to the final decree, spouses can sever their marital property interests and support arrangements by a legal separation decree or separate maintenance order. With such a decree/order, they are tax treated as unmarried.

Three. There is a distinction between legal separation and living apart. Legal separation establishes the date for severing marital property interests under local law, whereas "living apart" does not sever marital property interests.

Four. For live-aparts, there must be at least one dependent child in the household for one spouse to qualify as unmarried. If there are two or more children, with one or more living with each spouse, each spouse may qualify as unmarried . . . if the spouses live apart for the last 6 months of the year.

Four Possible Tax Filings

We will come back to Section 7703 later. We merely want to introduce you to it at this point, to convince you that while legally married under state law, you can be treated as unmarried under federal law. The significance of this tax treatment will become more apparent below.

For husband and wife headed for divorce, who are U.S. citizens, there are four possible tax-filing situations. These are:

1. Married Joint
2. Married Separate
3. Head of Household
4. Single Taxpayer

If you will look at your latest Form 1040, you will find these four choices in the block labeled: *Filing Status*. This status block is just below your name and address on page 1 of the 1040. An edited replica of this status block is presented in Figure 3.1. Note that there are actually *five* checkboxes on the official form. But we are only concerned with four of those checkboxes. We are dealing with divorce situations: not widows and widowers.

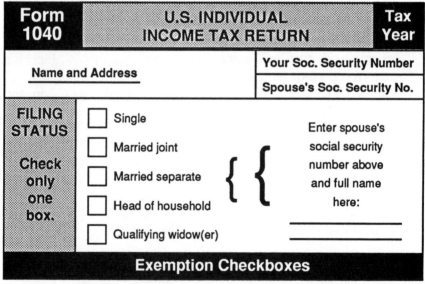

Fig. 3.1 - Filing Status Checkboxes on Form 1040

Note, too, that the instruction in the filing status says very specifically: *Check only one box*. This instruction means more than it says. It means that the filer must check only that one box for which he or she *qualifies*. For each checkbox, there is a different tax rate schedule. A filer cannot arbitrarily select a status that will give the lowest tax for the filing year.

If husband and wife are legally married on December 31, they may file a joint return. To do so, they may live together or they may not. It is immaterial. Many spouses going through divorce do not live together, yet file jointly. Thus, only one tax return is required.

Married persons, whether living together or not, can always file separately. They can do this by mutual agreement or by nonagreement. If by nonagreement, the spouse who files a separate return first sets the filing status for the other. The second-filing spouse must also file separately. Thus, there are two tax returns to be filed. Each "married separate" spouse checks the same status-box on his/her Form 1040.

Head of household also requires the filing of two returns (for husband and wife). The checkboxes, however, may differ — and often do. Two requirements must be met. One, the spouses must be unmarried at the end of year, *or considered so*. (This is where Section 7703 comes in.) The second requirement is that there must be at least one unmarried child living in the household.

Single status for tax filing applies only when one is single, or is considered so (under Section 7703 and other). The Form 1040 instruction booklet states—

Consider yourself single if on December 31 you were unmarried or separated from your spouse either by divorce or separate maintenance decree and you do not qualify for another filing status.

Thus, under the proper tax conditions, it is conceivable for married persons to file as two singles.

When Filing Required

When a joint return is not filed, there is the necessity (usually) for filing *two* returns: one "his" and one "hers." At least one spouse should file a return, whether the other does so or not. It is doubtful that each of the spouses would have sufficiently low income where neither would have to file.

Section 6012(a)(1)(A) requires the filing of an income tax return by—

*Every individual having for the taxable year gross income which equals or exceeds the exemption amount, except that a return shall not be required of an individual . . . who is not married (determined by applying section 7703) . . . and has a gross income of less than the sum of the **exemption amount** plus the basic **standard deduction** applicable to such an individual.* [Emphasis added.]

The term "every individual" means each and every person or spouse on his or her own. The problems of divorce and any despondency therewith are irrelevant. For starters, if one's gross income exceeds $5,000, he or she should be thinking of filing a return. This is an *individual* (per person) responsibility.

The term "exemption amount" is a per individual amount of $3,000 . . . **approximately**. There may be additional exemptions for each dependent: child, parent, relative, or other.

The term "standard deduction" is the amount of reportable income below which no tax is imposed. It applies after the exemption amount, and varies according to filing status. The standard deduction amounts are, approximately:

Married joint	8,000
Head of household	7,000
Single person	5,000
Married separate	4,000

We are forced to say "approximately" because all the amounts above are subject to change from year to year. Such are the consequences of inflation indexing and political "fine tuning." The more the standard deduction increases, the simpler it is to file.

For tax comparison purposes, the following generalizations apply to two-return filings:

One. For the same total taxable income, married filing separately produces the highest tax. Yet, married filing jointly does not produce the lowest tax. Other than tax considerations prevail to make the choice one or the other.

Two. One or both spouses qualifying as head of household produces the lowest total tax. Therefore, it behooves spouses with children to come to some tax agreement before divorce is final. The sharing of children can be tax advantageous for both.

Three. With or without children, it is possible for a living-apart married couple to file as two single taxpayers. A separate maintenance order or agreement could facilitate this. There are tax and other advantages for doing so.

Do you see now the importance of marital status when filing income tax returns? We lean towards two-return filings as being the more practical approach during the divorcing years.

Even if divorcing spouses (and their attorneys) haggle and bicker among themselves on family and other marital issues, it can be to their mutual advantage to agree on tax matters. They can agree, without having to file a joint return.

Married Filing Separately

A married person whose divorce is not yet final can file a separate return, with or without the knowledge or consent of the other spouse. Doing so means that each spouse is entirely on his/her own. There are separate tax accounting and separate tax liability by each, independent of the other. The only technical requirement is that the two separate returns be **consistent**. That is, both cannot ignore the same income and both cannot claim the same exemptions and same deductions.

The spouse who files a return first sets the consistency stage for the other spouse. Where there is likely overlapping of items on the two returns, it is best to assume a 50/50 split on such items. Simply take 50% of a controversial item on the premise of tax equality between the spouses.

As part of the overall consistency between the two returns, there is the *must itemize* requirement. This can present a tax problem. If one spouse itemizes his/her personal deductions (medical expenses, local taxes, mortgage interest, charitable contributions, etc.), the other spouse also must itemize. This must be done even though the "must itemize" spouse does not have enough deductions to come up to the standard deduction amount. The net effect is that the difference between the standard deduction and the "must" spouse's inadequate deductions is added to that spouse's taxable income.

Let us exemplify the must itemize problem. For illustration simplicity, assume that the standard deduction for married separate is $4,000. Suppose the "must" spouse's actual deductions are only $1,800. The difference of $2,200 (the $4,000 minus $1,800) is *added* to that spouse's taxable income. The reason for this is that the standard deduction amount is automatically built into the tax tables and tax schedules. In many cases, consequently, married filing separately can impose a tax disadvantage.

The selection of married-filing-separate status applies to any situation where no legal separation decree or separate maintenance order is in effect. Thus, the biggest advantage is that this status can be selected without any legal action being taken whatsoever. Furthermore, it can be selected unilaterally by either spouse.

When spouses file separately, the other spouse's *social security number* and full name must be shown. Quite often, one spouse becomes secretive and tries to hide his/her social security number from the other. If this is the case, look at your last joint return . . . if you kept a copy. If not, request a copy from the IRS. (Recall Form 4506 described on page 2-5.)

Married Living Apart

Let us swing back now to the special benefits of Section 7703(b): *Certain Married Individuals Living Apart.* Earlier, we quoted the key wording of this subsection. Therein, the term "certain" requires the presence of a *dependent child* in the household of one or the other of the married individuals. The term "child" includes stepchild, grandchild, and adopted child.

In substance, subsection 7703(b) permits a married person living apart, with a dependent child, to file as single or head of household, and not as married filing separately. There is a definite tax advantage in doing so. There is no "must itemize" requirement as in the case of married filing separately. There is no cross-referencing of the other spouse's social security number. and there's no co-liability feature as in the case of married filing jointly. Consequently, if married persons are indeed living apart in preparation for divorce, they should strive to meet the conditions of Section 7703(b).

There are four conditions that must be met, before married persons are tax treated as "living apart." These conditions are:

One. The spouses must actually and in fact live apart at all times during the last six months of the calendar year. That is, they must be able to document convincingly that they lived in two separate households commencing on or before June 30 of the live-apart year.

Two. There must be at least one dependent child for whom one or both spouses contributed more than 50% of that child's total support. That is, the child must be a minor, or attending school full time, or be disabled or unemployed.

Three. The dependent child's principal place of abode must be in the household of one spouse or the other "more than" one-half of the taxable year. That is, the custodial spouse must document the child's live-in dates comprising more than six months' abode time, each year. For those states which prescribe "joint custody" (i.e., 50/50 by each parent), alternate custodial years can be mutually satisfying to both spouses as parents.

Four. The custodial spouse (and parent) must furnish more than one-half the cost of maintaining the household for himself/herself *and* for the dependent child. That is, the household cost (rent, mortgage, taxes, insurance, utilities, food, repairs) must be documented for the entire year, of which the custodial spouse must contribute more than 50%.

If there is only one dependent child living with one of the living-apart spouses, that particular spouse—

   . . . *shall not be considered as married* [Sec. 7703(b), very last phrase].

A person "not considered married" (for tax purposes) may file as a single person or head of household. We'll discuss the difference more fully in Chapter 6: Child Dependency.

How must the other living-apart spouse file?

A living-apart spouse with no dependent child in his/her custody must file as "married filing separately."

Thus, we have a situation where two living apart spouses may show filing statuses on their tax returns that are quite different from each other.

If there are two dependent children, one in the household of each living-apart spouse, both spouses may file as single or both may file as head of household. This is a much more advantageous tax situation.

When "Deemed Unmarried"

The living-apart rule is also called the "deemed unmarried" rule. That which is "deemed" is that the divorce will eventually finalize and that the spouses will not cohabit again.

The deemed unmarried theory is applicable only to federal tax law. It is a convenience and incentive for spouses in the throes of divorce to file their tax returns on time. It is not a substitute for divorce law in the state of domicile of the separating spouses.

There are three other deemed unmarried situations which apply to federal tax law (and, in many cases, to state tax law, too). These situations are:

1. Legal separation decree
2. Separate maintenance order
3. Nonresident alien spouse

Legal separation is a court decree whereby the spouses are mandated to live apart separately, before all details of the marital dissolution process (particularly, property settlement) are finalized. This is sometimes called "bifurcation" of the marriage. All marital rights and burdens between husband and wife cease, leaving property rights still to be severed. Legal separation is sought primarily where there are no children, or where the children, if any, are adults, and where each spouse is separately employed and self-supporting. Generally, a legal separation decree has all the earmarks of a "final" if the spouses may remarry other persons.

Separate maintenance is also a court decree which accomplishes much the same as legal separation, but there are minor children involved. Or, one of the spouses is unemployed or unemployable, and needs the marital residence as a transitional domicile for himself/herself and/or for the minor children. Usually, a separate maintenance order is accompanied by a specified amount for spousal support and another specified amount for child support. Under a separate maintenance order, neither spouse can remarry until a final decree of divorce is issued.

A nonresident alien is a person who is not a citizen of the United States, and who, for at least one day of the year, physically resided outside of the United States. The problem with nonresident alien marriages is that tax matters get drawn into highly complex features of international law. Different marital customs and practices prevail, such as: multiple spouses, extramarital rights, property rights, discrimination on the basis of sex, pooled income clans, and religious teachings of children. A U.S. citizen (whether or not a resident) or a U.S. resident (whether or not a citizen) married to a nonresident alien is generally deemed unmarried for tax filing purposes. Married filing jointly is not allowed.

The section of the tax code which expressly identifies the three deemed unmarried situations above is Section 2(b)(2): *Determination of status*. The pertinent portions are—

For purposes of [tax filings] . . .
(B) an individual who is legally separated from his spouse under a decree of divorce or of separate maintenance shall not be considered as married;
(C) a taxpayer shall be considered as not married at the close of his taxable year if at any time during the taxable year his spouse is a nonresident alien.

Again, the point that we are trying to make is that the deemed unmarried rules [Sec. 2(b)(2)(B) **and** Sec. 7703(a)(2) permit those persons whose divorce is not final-final to file separate federal returns as single or head of household. Either of these filings is preferable to married joint or married separate.

IRS's "Forcing" Stance

Two spouses filing separate returns as singles, or filing separately as heads of household, pay less total tax than if they filed "married separate." The greater the total income of the two spouses, the greater the revenue differential when filing married separate. For this reason, the IRS invariably will try to force separated spouses into filing married separate returns. This is "easy money" for aggressive IRS agents who like to take advantage of other people's marital woes. As depicted in Figure 3.2, an IRS agent's power to say "No" can force upon the spouses an involuntary filing status.

The most common situation for forcing married separate returns upon separated spouses involves an *interlocutory decree* of divorce. The legal wording in such a decree may have all the earmarks of living apart, legal separation, separate maintenance, spousal support, child support, property division, and so on. Yet, it is **not** a deemed unmarried situation. The reason is that an interlocutory has only a temporary or provisional effect. Its purpose is to allow the spouses to work out their differences if they can, and/or to allow them to reconcile their marriage if they choose. Consequently, an interlocutory lacks the anticipatory finality of divorce, as in the case of a legal separation decree or a separate maintenance order.

Other cases when the IRS forces married separate filings on the two spouses involve ambiguities in state laws or conflicts between state law for spouses living in different states. Often, spouses will live apart under a legal separation *agreement*. Such an arrangement is not a court mandate although it may be, and often is, court sanctioned. An "agreement" is not a judicial mandate, preparatory to absolute dissolution of the marriage. An agreement can be abrogated by the parties upon reconciliation and resumption of cohabitation.

A temporary support order, combined with a temporary restraining order prohibiting one spouse from entering the marital domicile, is just that. It is "temporary." It does not create a judicial separation or establish a permanent status of rights for the future.

Fig. 3.2 - Key Points for Qualifying as "Deemed Unmarried"

A separate maintenance decree based on extreme cruelty, for example, is not, per se, an alteration of the original basket of marital rights. The implication is that when the conditions of cruelty and battery are removed, the marriage will resume. Therefore, the parties are deemed married.

The fine points of state law as interpreted by IRS agents are the greatest obstacle to separated spouses filing as singles or heads of household. Although IRS agents have no expertise as legal translators, they do have the bureaucratic power to say "No." They get away with it, unfortunately, because most state court orders are prepared without federal tax consequences in mind.

Filing as Single Persons

If there are no children involved, spouses undergoing divorce pay less tax if they can file as two single persons. If they cannot file as singles, they must file married separate and pay the highest tax. The advantage of married filing separately is that the subsequent filing of a joint return is not ruled out. If the spouses are communicative and cooperative, they can file jointly (via an amended return). Filing jointly produces less total tax than married separate, but a higher tax than two singles.

Most individuals in the throes of divorce inherently understand that filing as a single person is a simple, hassle-free way to go. If they are living apart and intend to remain so, why not file as single? We'll now tell you why you cannot.

In the Tax Court case of *Hale v. IRS*, TC Memo 1982-527, the couple were married (legally) for less than one year. One day, the wife left her husband and ceased all communication with him. For 12 years he tried to locate his wife, even reporting her to the police as a "missing person." There was no evidence of foul play. Apparently, she was just moving from place to place to avoid her husband locating her. She had taken on a completely different lifestyle of her own. The husband did not file for divorce because he had no address for serving legal papers on her. So, he filed his own tax returns each year as a single person.

Guess what happened?

The IRS said "No"; the husband said "Yes." So they went to Tax Court. The Tax Court also said "No." The rationale was that although the husband had plenty of evidence that his wife had abandoned him, he had no judicial decree (court order) that altered his original marital status. Until he obtained such a decree, he had to file his tax returns as married separate. He also had to pay back taxes, plus interest, for *three* of the prior 12 years that he filed as single. Because he filed on time each year, the IRS was limited to three years for back collections [65011(a)].

Until divorce is finalized, the opportunity to file as single persons is rather limited. The most practical way to file as two singles is to get a legal separation decree (if both are self-supporting) or a separate maintenance order (if one spouse requires support from the other). The decree or order must be a legal instrument under applicable state law. It also should be clear and specific as to the finality of divorce intent.

As we've seen in the Hale case above, the mere living apart of spouses — regardless of the length of time — does not automatically qualify such persons to file as single status. For one spouse or the other to file as tax single, there must be at least one dependent child. The spouse/parent filing as "single" pays all or most of the necessary child support, but does not house the child in his/her own household.

Head of Household Status

The "head of household" status is the least understood marital status because its technical qualifications are narrow and specific. The qualifications vary considerably from what one ordinarily thinks of as being head of household. At least one minor child or elderly parent must be involved.

This status is the most misused because it produces the lowest total tax for "split incomes." Consequently, there is great temptation to use it, even though one does not meet all of the technical qualifications.

There is a specific statutory definition of head of household. It is embodied in Section 2: *Definitions and Special Rules*, of the Internal Revenue Code. In pertinent part, Section 2(b)(1): *Head of Household*, says—

For purposes of this subtitle [Income Taxes] *an individual shall be considered a head of a household if, and only if, such individual is not married at the close of his taxable year . . . and either—*
(A) maintains as his home a household which constitutes for more than one-half of such taxable year the principal place of abode, as a member of such household, of—
(i) a [child] *of the taxpayer . . . but if such* [child] *is married at the close of the taxpayer's taxable year, only if the taxpayer is entitled to a* [dependency] *deduction . . . for such person . . . or*

(B) maintains a household which constitutes . . . the principal place of abode of the father or mother of the taxpayer, if the taxpayer is entitled to a [dependency] deduction . . . for such father or mother.
For purposes of this paragraph, an individual shall be considered as maintaining a household only if over half of the cost of maintaining the household during the taxable year is furnished by such individual.

Note particularly above the phrase: "if, and only if." It was placed in bold type for emphasis. The "only if" means that if any of the qualifications are not met, the head of household status cannot be used. In a nutshell, the qualifications are:

1. be unmarried or "deemed" so
2. furnish over half the cost of maintaining a household
3. have a "qualifying member" in the household.

The persons who qualify as a "qualifying member" are described in Figure 3.3.
   A "household" is one's place of abode. It may be an owned home, a rented apartment, a mobile home, or any form of customary accommodation for living, sleeping, and working. By deductive reasoning, head of household precludes any presence of the other spouse.
   Furnishing over half the cost of maintaining a household means making direct payments for property taxes, mortgage payments (or rental payments), insurance, utilities, repairs, maintenance, furniture, furnishings, appliances, landscaping, and the like. Also included is the cost of food consumed on the premises and any necessary domestic help. Household costs do *not* include clothing, education, transportation, medical treatment, life insurance, entertainment, and vacations for household members.

Changing Filing Status

One's selection of tax-filing status is not forever cast in concrete. Under certain conditions, you can change your mind after a return is

PERSON	REQUIREMENTS	COMMENT
Un- married Child	Must live in household more than six months (except for vacation and school). Need not be a dependent.	May be your child, step- child, foster child, or grandchild. If not a de- pendent, enter name alongside filing status.
Married Child	Must live in household the entire year (except for vacation and school). Must be a sole dependent without support from others (including the child's spouse).	May be married child, step-child, foster child, or grandchild. Enter first name on "exemptions" line.
Parent	Parents must be primarily depen- dent upon filer for total support. Filer must pay more than one-half the cost of keeping up "a home".	Parent need not live in same household as filer.
Other Relative	Any blood relative counts if that relative: (a) lives in household entire year, and (b) is solely dependent upon filer.	May be brother, sister, in- law, parent, grandparent, uncle, aunt, or any other person.

Fig. 3.3 - Qualifying Member(s) for Head-of-Household Status

filed. You have up to three years after the due date of a return in which to do so. If the original return was timely filed, any change in filing status will also be treated as timely filed.

The way to change your filing status is to file Form 1040X: *Amended U.S. Individual Income Tax Return.* That is, you can "amend" your originally filed return for any number of reasons, including change in filing status. For filing status changes, see Figure 3.4. Note that there are two rows of checkboxes there. In each row of boxes, only one box can be checked.

In Figure 3.4, the "original return" row refers to the tax return initially filed for the specific tax year for which the change is to be effective. The "this return" row applies to Form 1040X. Only one tax year at a time can be changed on Form 1040X.

For example, if your original return was checked "married separate," you could later file an amended return claiming single status, married joint, or head of household. Amending a return does not "red flag" it for audit, if your facts are correct and you do so in

Form 1040X	AMENDED U.S. INDIVIDUAL INCOME TAX RETURN	Tax Year

Name, Social Security Number
Old Address; New Address

FILING STATUS CLAIMED

	Single	Married Joint	Married Separate	Head of Household
On Original Return: ▶	☐	☐	☐	☐
On This Return: ▶	☐	☐	☐	☐

- -

Note: You cannot change from joint to separate returns after the due date has passed.

**Income and Deductions
Tax Liability
Payments and Credits**

Fig. 3.4 - Filing Status Checkboxes on Form 1040X

good faith. If two or more tax years are to be changed, there must be a separate Form 1040X for each such year.

There is only one exception to the privilege of changing your filing status. This is stated in a special note on Form 1040X (shown in Figure 3.4), namely:

You cannot change from joint to separate returns after the due date has passed.

The reason for this prohibition is that a joint return is an *elective return*: it is not mandatory. As such, the election becomes irrevocable after the due date (April 15) for filing the original return

A joint return constitutes a binding election. It is "binding" in that tax liability is fully enforceable upon either spouse . . . whichever one has the money, or whichever one can be reached the easier. This binding liability holds long after a divorce is final. The filing of separate returns avoids any and all joint tax liability.

4

SEPARATE RETURNS

For Best Tax Protection Long Term, Separate Spousal Returns Should Be Filed. Crucial In This Regard Is The "Timely Filing" Of These Returns On Or Before April 15. Extensions And Delays Can Cause The IRS To Assert Married Joint Or Married Separate, Whichever Produces The Higher Revenue. The Best Legal Basis For Separate Returns Is A Clearly Worded "Separate Maintenance Order." Such An Order (Or Decree) Permits Filing As Single Or Head Of Household. It Sets The Stage For Proper Allocation Of Tax And Fiscal Affairs Between The Spouses. Any Spousal Support Paid Is Tax Deductible By The Payer.

When petition for divorce has been filed, and the spouses live physically separated, the most prudent tax choice is to file completely separate returns. We say "most prudent" because, with but few exceptions, the continuation of filing jointly invariably creates tax inequities for one spouse or the other. The whole concept of jointness and mutual trust falls apart when the spouses begin living separately on their own.

The filing of two separate returns is more complicated than filing one joint return. (You will see why this is so, as we progress through this chapter.) The longer a couple has been married before separating, the more complex is the filing of separate returns. Much more "spousal separation" tax accounting has to be done. Though difficult for the separation year, the extra effort is worth it. Much tax shock, trauma, and hysteria can be avoided later on.

For spouses in the throes of divorce, the dangers in a joint return seldom surface until several years later. "Several" can mean anywhere from three to six years. If tax deficiencies show up, the penalties and interest can far exceed initial tax.

A "Don't Do Joint" Example

Here is an illustration of what can happen in real life. In 1992, the "tacit consent" rule was upheld where a separated spouse did not sign a joint return for 1986. The separated (nonconsenting) spouse was held solely liable for a major tax deficiency by the filing spouse *six years later*! The filing spouse was the husband.

The husband filed a joint return by writing in the wife's signature. The wife (living separately) had carefully warned her husband that she would not sign a joint return for 1986 because she was going to file a separate return on her own. She did not do so because she could not locate her W-2 at filing time.

The wife in this case was a nurse who received W-2 income with withholdings commensurate with her marital status. The W-2 was sent to her marital address, where she was not living. Divorce was in process but not final. There was no separate maintenance or legal separation order. The husband intercepted the W-2 and attached it to the joint return.

The husband was self-employed and not subject to withholdings. He was required to make estimated tax prepayments, but he did not do so.

The husband greatly exaggerated his self-employment business expenses. As a consequence, the joint return showed a refund of the entire amount of the wife's withholdings: approximately $3,000. The refund check was made payable to both spouses jointly. The husband again signed the wife's name, deposited the check, and immediately withdrew the $3,000.

Three years later, the 1986 return was audited by the IRS. A $5,000 tax deficiency was assessed . . . plus approximately $4,000 in penalties and interest. In the meantime, the husband had died.

From whom did the IRS collect the $9,000?

Answer: The nonconsenting spouse (the wife). Altogether, the joint return cost her nearly $12,000 ($3,000 of withholdings, $5,000 tax deficiency, and $4,000 in penalties and interest). She contested the matter into Tax Court.

The Tax Court took the position that, because she failed to file a separate return (for 1986) after warning her husband that she was going to do so, she "tacitly consented and acquiesced to" the joint return. It made no difference that her husband intercepted her W-2; she could have obtained a duplicate from her employer. Since the due date for the 1986 joint return had long passed, she could not go back and refile separately. [*H.J. Crew*. TC Memo 1992-535.]

This is a clear-cut case of tax inequity between separated spouses. Nevertheless, under joint return rules, co-liability is a statutory mandate. A spouse who does not willingly consent to a joint return must take positive, specific separate action on his or her own. Doing nothing is the equivalent of tacit consent.

Simplest Option: Married Separate

The above is a specific case where "married filing separate" returns should have been made. At least by the wife.

She did, indeed file a married separate return. But it was filed *after* the April 15 due date. Expecting a refund on her own, she had an automatic 60-day extension to June 15. She filed her return in early June. The husband filed the forged joint return just prior to April 15. He was diligent about this.

The tax rules in this situation are pretty clear. A joint return filed on time cannot be changed by filing a separate return after the due date has passed. Specifically on point is IRS Regulation 1.6013-1(a): *Separate returns shall not be made by the spouses after the time for filing the return of either spouse has expired.*

Cross-referencing on a married separate return is a "must" requirement. In the case above, the wife followed instructions and gave on her return the social security number and name of her husband. This triggered the IRS to check the husband's return. When the IRS did so, they rejected the wife's separate return in its entirety. Realizing there was a tax contradiction between the spouses, the IRS homed in on the forged joint return. Upon audit, the husband's return was found to contain gross errors. Hence, the deficiency assessment plus penalties and interest.

There is a strong message in the above "don't do" example. If you intend to file married separate, **do so on time!** This means on or before April 15. Do not rely on any extensions, automatic or expressly approved. When there are any prospects of divorce whatsoever, timely filing gives one the greatest tax protection.

The biggest advantage of filing a married separate return is that either spouse can take the action unilaterally. Furthermore, the filing can be done without a petition for divorce, and without moving out of the marital residence. Unlike a joint return, mutual consent is not required. The spouse who files first sets the tax stage for the other. This is not common knowledge among spouses who have been filing jointly for many years. Consequently, married filing separate is the simplest way to avoid being held "tax hostage" by a noncooperative spouse.

"Living Apart" Tax Problems

We spent a good portion of Chapter 3 discussing Section 7703(b) of the tax code. This section, recall, is titled: *Certain Married Individuals Living Apart*. This has become known as the deemed-unmarried-by-living-apart rule. It requires at least one dependent child in one of the spouse's household, and requires that the spouses live apart for the last six months of the year.

There is also another living-apart rule, namely: Section 66(a). This rule is titled: *Treatment of Community Income Where Spouses Live Apart*. The essence of this rule is that if the spouses live apart "at all times during the calendar year," and do not transfer any community income between themselves, they may file as other than joint . . . under certain conditions.

There are a lot of tax problems with these living apart rules. The requirements are quite technical, and convincing documentation is needed. Upon the slightest misstep, the IRS will deny single or head-of-household status. Married separate is then imposed upon both spouses (to produce the highest revenue).

When spouses take to living apart voluntarily, it is often a gradual, trial-type arrangement. There are visits to pick up clothing, papers, furniture, and other items. There are attempts at reconciliation. The filing of a petition for divorce is put off. As a consequence, there is no specific date of separation that can be third-party documented. A clearly defined — verifiable — separation date is a tax accounting benchmark.

Where there is a child (or children) involved, there are matters of temporary custody, support, and visitation. The child (or children) may live part-time with each parent. Good tax documentation requires a detailed diary of each overnight stay, and an itemized listing of actual money spent on each child. Parents going through divorce seldom do these things.

Another living-apart tax problem has to do with money exchanges between the spouses. Money transfers are needed for house payments, utility bills, medical expenses, spousal support, investment activities, and the continuation of any family trade or business. Not all of the money transfers are tax accountable, but some are. Seldom is the proper documentation available. Without documentation, all money transactions between spouses are treated as personal gifts. They are not tax recognized.

We are trying to make a very important point here. You must use **extreme caution** when relying on the living-apart-deemed-unmarried rules. The IRS mentality is not known for its compassion and understanding of real life situations. To avoid being IRS-deemed "married filing separate" (instead of single or head of household), we urge that you take matters more into your hands. If you are going to live apart, file a petition for divorce. At least this will establish a documented separation date.

A "Do-It-Yourself" Option

If divorce is likely to occur within a three-year period, there is a do-it-yourself option that could be workable. It requires that each spouse be separately employed and self-sustaining. It also requires civil communication between the spouses for drawing up terms for their separate maintenance. If there are any children involved, the parents agree civilly on matters of (temporary) custody and visitation.

Suppose a petition for divorce is filed in the proper court, together with a *stipulation* of separate maintenance. A "stipulation" is a concession as to certain facts and conditions which cannot be refuted later. Would this arrangement permit the spouses to each tax file independently of the other, as single or head of household?

Yes, we think it would . . . under the right legalities.

Suppose that the spouses had voluntarily separated, and were indeed living apart in separate residences of their own. Each is separately employed and requires (for the time being) no support payments from the other. Prior to December 31 of the tax year, one of the spouses takes it upon himself (or herself) to file a court petition for dissolution of marriage. Incorporated in the petition is the stipulation that, until further order of the court, the spouses will support and maintain themselves separately. Upon "proof of service" on the respondent spouse, the petition/stipulation becomes an obligation imposed by law. If proof of service was established before December 31, there would be no "last six months," nor any other living-apart time requirement.

Because divorce is so common these days, many states now have standard divorce petition forms. These legal forms are listed under "Family Law Forms" sold by stationery stores and printing shops. For instructional and identification purposes, an edited sample petition is presented in Figure 4.1. Note that all of the essentials are covered in succinct terms.

The entries on the petition form are rather routine, except for the stipulation terms. There is no need to hire an attorney for this one form. You could prepare it yourself; many spouses do. All you're trying to do is get the legal ball rolling before December 31. There are paralegals who will help you for a modest fee.

If the standard petition form available in your state does not provide space for the stipulation that you want, you can attach a sheet and make reference to it in the petition. In most standard forms there is a space or checkbox for "other." Insert the words: See Stipulation Attached. Then, in a short statement say that—

IT IS HEREBY STIPULATED AND CONFIRMED by and between the parties hereto that:
1. Each party shall support and maintain himself/herself separately from the other;
2. The party housing a child (if any) shall support and maintain that child as a dependent;

```
┌─────────────────────────────────────────────┬──────────────────────┐
│ Name, Address, Telephone                     │                      │
│ • Petitioner (in pro se)                     │                      │
│ • Attorney for petitioner                    │   For Court Use      │
├─────────────────────────────────────────────┴──────────────────────┤
│ SUPERIOR COURT OF _____, COUNTY OF _____                  │
├─────────────────────────────────────────────┬──────────────────────┤
│ Petitioner _____             │ Case No. _____    │
│ and                                          │                      │
│ Respondent _____             │   PETITION           │
│                                              │   (DIVORCE)          │
└─────────────────────────────────────────────┴──────────────────────┘
```

THIS PETITION IS FOR:

1. Dissolution of marriage pursuant to Civil Code section(s) _____ .

2. __(petitioner or respondent)__ has been a resident of this state for at least 6 months and of this county for at least 3 months immediately preceding the filing of this petition.

FACTS CONCERNING THIS MARRIAGE:

1. Social Security Numbers

     Husband _____

     Wife   _____

2. Date and place of marriage _____

3. Date and place of separation _____

4. The number of years from date of marriage to date of separation is _____ years, _____ months, and _____ days.

5. There are _____ children of this marriage, as follows:

    Name   Birthdate   Age   Sex

FACTS CONCERNING CAUSE OF ACTION:

1. The cause of this petition is due to

    ☐ Irreconcilable differences in marriage

    ☐ Reprehensible conduct of _____

    ☐ Other _____

IMMEDIATE CONSENT IS SOUGHT FOR:

1. Upon proof of service to respondent, petitioner requests this court's immediate consent to the following:

    ☐ Stipulation of separate maintenance (attached hereto and incorporated within)

    ☐ Temporary custody of children be awarded to _____

    ☐ Other _____

Dated: _____   _____
                        (signature of petitioner)
                        TYPED OR PRINTED NAME

I declare under penalty of perjury that the foregoing is true and correct and that this declaration is executed on _____ at _____ .

                        _____
                        (signature of petitioner)
                        TYPED OR PRINTED NAME

Fig. 4.1 - Edited Format/Contents of "Routine" Divorce Petition

3. Each party shall maintain his/her own records and shall prepare and file his/her own tax returns independent of the other; and

4. This stipulation shall be binding upon both parties until, upon proper hearing, it is changed by order of the court.

Or, words to this effect.

The whole idea of the petition/stipulation is to get something "up front" in writing that becomes a third-party document for tax purposes. Such documents are always more acceptable to the IRS than spousal declarations which are prepared after the IRS comes on the scene to demand more money.

Your Best Option: SMO

The letters S-M-O stand for: **Separate Maintenance Order.** This is a written order or decree signed by a judge, magistrate, or commissioner having legal jurisdiction over family law matters. The order must follow a petition for divorce, and be issued upon "due notice and hearing." This means that both spouses have the opportunity to state their positions in open court.

The SMO hearing is not a substitute for, nor does it bypass, an alimony hearing, child support hearing, property disclosure hearing, property settlement, or other controversial issue. Hearings, if any, on these matters come later. The sole purpose of the SMO hearing is to alter the marital relationship and set the conditions for the separate maintenance of each spouse, so that the spouses can be treated as unmarrieds for tax purposes.

We do not recommend that you attempt to get an SMO on your own. The main reason is that it is *not* a routine divorce matter under most state laws. There is no standard form for it. You will need an attorney, and we urge that you get one. Not all attorneys, however, understand the function and purpose of an SMO. So, you'll have to tax educate them.

What you want to do is achieve *full compliance* with Section 7703(a)(2) of the Internal Revenue Code. To refresh your recall on the wording, it is—

*An individual legally separated from his spouse under a decree
... of separate maintenance shall not be considered as married.*

A "decree" is an order having the force of law. It is a judicial
decision; it is not an agreement or stipulation by the parties involved.

We want you and your attorney to focus on the phrase: *shall
not be considered as married.* If you are not considered as married,
you cannot tax file as married joint or as married separate. You
must file either as single or head of household. That is, with an
SMO each spouse must file completely independently of the other.
You file as though you were never married. Tax-amount-wise and
tax-liability-wise, you are much better off. Without doubt, an SMO
is your best defense (short of the final divorce decree itself) against
the eagerness of the IRS for maximum revenue.

A properly prepared SMO does two things for you. One, it
establishes a legal separation date for tax reference purposes. From
this date on, all recordkeeping and accounting are the responsibility
of each spouse independently.

The second thing that an SMO does is to set spousal support
arrangements. This enables one spouse to pay the other periodic
amounts of money . . . and *get a tax deduction for it*! That is, the
payer spouse gets a tax deduction. The payee (recipient) spouse gets
a tax inclusion. Thus, the SMO legitimizes tax shifting between
spouses. In all of the other deemed unmarried options, the transfers
of money from one spouse to the other are considered gifts. They
are neither tax deductible nor tax includible. This one tax shifting
feature alone makes the cost and effort of getting an SMO well
worthwhile.

So that you (and your attorney) can more fully appreciate the
power and flexibility of an SMO, we present Figure 4.2. It
summarizes in pictorial form the tax essence of being deemed
unmarried.

Tax Contents of SMO

We want to stress again that we are urging a separate
maintenance order strictly for tax-filing purposes. It is so that each
spouse can come within the statutory provision for treatment as

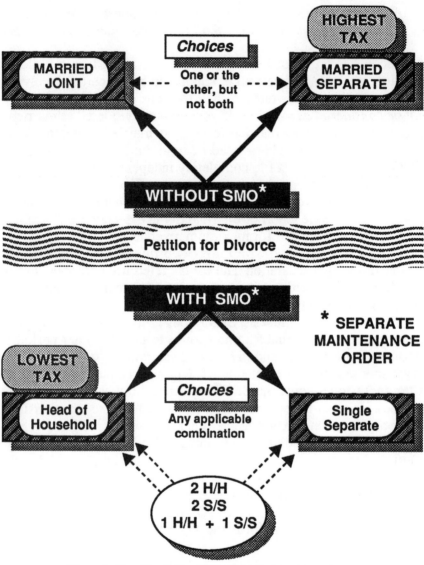

Fig. 4.2 - Tax Flexibility With SMO Before Final Decree

unmarried. It is not a legal dissolution of marriage. The spouses are still legally married under the law of their state of domicile. They are merely treated as unmarried for federal tax purposes. Both spouses can benefit from the arrangement, as should be self-evident in Figure 4.2.

Because we are discussing federal tax law (not state family law), there are certain required contents of a successful separate maintenance order. The term "successful" means capable of withstanding an IRS audit challenge to each spouse's return, several years after the divorce petition.

The key ingredient of a separate maintenance order for tax purposes is the legal date of separation and judicial language requiring the spouses to maintain themselves separately. The clear implication must be that the marital rights are altered and that divorce will ultimately ensue. Included is spousal support where one spouse has no viable means of support on his or her own. Also included is a prohibition against each spouse incurring debts and liabilities against the other. As a judicial mandate, the spouses shall live separate tax accounting lives on their own.

An overall listing of the tax points to be covered in an SMO is presented in Figure 4.3. Note that we list 10 specific points. We urge that you take a moment and read (or skim read) each one.

Making Proper Allocations

The first year of filing separately will commence a new tax experience. The new experience is the separation from prior joint returns and joint accounts various items into "His" and "Hers." Doing so is called: *allocation*. The first year for allocating all tax information is the *separation year*. Thereafter, adjustments are made each year so that the allocation process is fair and proper.

There are three conceptual approaches to the proper allocation of tax information between separate spouses. These are diagrammed in Figure 4.4 as I, II, and III. Note that the date of separation is the pivotal accounting point.

Part I of Figure 4.4 refers to the support and maintenance of the individual spouses themselves. (Support and maintenance of children will be discussed in Chapter 6.) Up to the date of separation, each spouse gets an equal 50/50 split of all applicable tax deductions, credits, etc. If only one spouse is working, the income of that spouse is also split 50/50. After the date of separation, the

ITEM	TAX POINT	REASON
1.	Date of petition (and case number) in proper court for dissolution of marriage.	Establishes legality under governing state law.
2.	Date of hearing on motion for separate maintenance order.	Establishes tax-filing intent by petitioner or respondent, whichever seeks the order.
3.	Confirmed date of physical/legal separation, with order prescribing continuation of such.	Fixes a legal date for allocating pertinent tax issues.
4.	Setting of spousal support, if any, in dollars per month, commencing on a specific date.	Tax deductible by payer; tax includible by receiver.
5.	Full name of each spouse with separate address, social security number, home/office phone number.	Facilitates cross checking of separate returns by tax preparers and IRS auditors.
6.	Treatment of marital income, deductions, and credits prior to legal date of separation.	Usually split 50/50 where prior year return was joint.
7.	Prohibition against the incurrence of debts and liabilities by either spouse against the other.	Avoids hassle on proper tax deduction for debts paid; exception for marital residence.
8.	Description and (temporary) treatment of joint property after legal date of separation.	Usually split 50/50 where prior year return was joint.
9.	Designation that medical, insurance, home, car, or other payments by one spouse on behalf of the other be treated as additional spousal support by the paying spouse.	Avoids uncanny tax traps; amounts deductible by payer as alimony; certain amounts paid are tax deductible by receiving spouse.
10.	Specify that each spouse file a separate tax return on his/her own, and that all "proper allocations" be made.	Avoid any mention or implication of joint return. A joint return cannot be changed after its due date for filing.

Fig. 4.3 - Tax Points in a Separate Maintenance Order

income of the working spouse is reduced by the amount of support paid to/for the nonworking spouse.

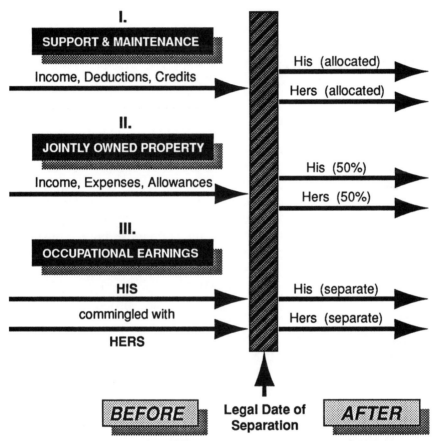

Fig. 4.4 - Concepts of Tax Accounting by Separated Spouses

Part II of Figure 4.4 pertains to the income and expenses (including allowances, such as depreciation, depletion, and amortization) of that property owned jointly between the spouses. Since a separate maintenance order does *not* include property settlement, the tax accounting for jointly owned property is allocated 50/50 after the date of separation. This allocation continues so, until all marital property is distributed.

Part III of Figure 4.4 treats those situations in which each spouse is earning income in separate occupations. This is the "two-working" spousal situation which is quite common today. If the earnings are more or less uniform throughout the separation year, each spouse tracks and accounts for his/her own earnings both before and after the date of separation. This is so, regardless of whether the spouses earn equally or unequally. If the earnings are derived from a husband-wife business, they are treated as in Part II: 50/50 each.

Allocation Example 1

For illustration purposes, consider that the date of separation is May 1. This means that there are four months of marital accounting, and eight months of separate accounting in the separation year. Assume that there are interest, dividends, and capital accounts which are owned jointly. Assume that the marital residence is occupied by the wife for the entire year, but the husband pays the taxes and interest thereon. They own jointly a piece of rental income property. The wife is employed and is subject to W-2 withholdings. The husband is self-employed and is subject to estimated tax prepayments. What are the "proper allocation" problems here?

Even if the spouses are both dutiful, and tax communicate with each other amicably, the IRS's Big Computer can really foul things up. Its mismatching of social security numbers and payer reportings will drive you wild.

For example, all payers of interest and dividends on joint accounts must report same to the IRS on Forms 1099-INT and 1099-DIV. These forms are indexed to the social security number of the person first named on a joint account, more often the husband. The IRS has a computer-matching program called "CP-2000." The purpose of CP-2000 is to check the husband's return to see if he reports *all* the interest and dividends. How does he report his income when the wife is allocated her share? Assume that there is $1,500 in interest and $900 in dividend income.

Answer: The husband uses Schedule B, Form 1040 (Interest and Dividend Income) and reports as follows:

Interest Income	$1,500
less 50% to spouse	(750)
(Name & Soc. Sec. No.)	
Dividend Income	$ 900
less 50% to spouse	(450)
(Name & Soc. Sec. No.)	

In this manner, the computer could be satisfied. The husband nets out the wife's 50% portion so that he pays tax only on his share. The computer could then cross-check on the wife, to see that she reports her share. If the wife doesn't report her share, the IRS contacts the husband for an explanation . . . and documents.

Allocation Example 2

Now, assume that the property tax on the marital residence is $1,200 for the separation year, and that the mortgage interest is $9,000. The husband has all of the canceled checks as proof of his payment. How are these items allocated?

Answer: The husband *and* wife use Schedule A, Form 1040 (Itemized Deductions) and report as follows:

	Husband	*Wife*
Real estate taxes		
• 4 mo (50% each)	$ 200	$ 200
• 8 mo (100% H)	800	-0-
Mortgage interest		
• 4 mo (50% each)	1,500	1,500
• 8 mo (100% H)	6,000	-0-
Totals	$8,500	$1,700

The problem with this scenario is that, again, the IRS computer will foul things up. All interest paid on mortgages is reported to the IRS on Form 1098: *Mortgage Interest Statement.* Mortgage companies have their own computers and they, too, will foul things up. Invariably, the husband's social security number will be on Form 1098. So, the *wife* is the one to "allocation fight" the IRS.

The computer matching situation is even more complicated for jointly owned rental property. Particularly if neither spouse lives in the rental property and it produces income of its own. In this case, both spouses split-report 50/50 all rental income, expenses, and depreciation. However, if one spouse has to pay additional amounts out of his or her separate (nonrental) income, the spouse who pays gets the deduction. But, again, there's a long, drawn-out computer allocation fight with the IRS.

Allocation Example 3

In still another vein, assume that the spouses bought 100 shares of stock before their separation, which cost them $10,000. The stock is now worth $4,000. That is, they have a $6,000 capital loss. They mutually agree to sell the stock after separation. How is the loss allocated?

Answer: Each spouse uses Schedule D, Form 1040 (Capital Gains and Losses) and reports as follows—

	Sales Price	*Cost Basis*	*Loss*
50 shares	$2,000	$5,000	($3,000)

Simple enough?

No, there's a catch here.

Ordinarily, Schedule D allows up to $3,000 as a maximum loss writeoff. But the fine print instructions say—

$1,500 if married and filing a separate return

Here's a case where "deemed unmarried" does not apply. The spouses were married when they bought the stock. It retains its community character, even though it was sold after the spouses separated. So, instead of each spouse getting a $3,000 loss writeoff, each gets only $1,500. This is just one example of the tax traps that divorcing spouses must anticipate.

However, if the spouses split the stock 50/50 before their date of separation, and had it re-issued as 50 shares in each separate name, each would then have his/her own separate property. Upon sale, each would get the maximum $3,000 capital loss writeoff. Thus, they would get *two* $3,000 loss writeoffs instead of one.

Treatment of Spousal Support

One of the complications that arise in preparing separate returns is the treatment of spousal support. If it is not handled properly, it is treated as an interspousal gift: not deductible by the payer; not reportable by the recipient. However, let us illustrate the proper treatment with two different examples: A — both spouses working, and B — one spouse working.

For Case A, assume that the wife earns $12,000 from employment wages, and that the husband earns $36,000 net from his self-employment business. They were living together four months of the year. The separate maintenance order directs that the husband pay the wife $1,000 per month as spousal support. How are their two (separate) incomes reported?

Answer: On Form 1040, page 1, the wife reports as follows—

W-2 wages	12,000
Alimony received (8 mo)	8,000
Total income	20,000

On a separate Form 1040, page 1, the husband reports—

Business income	36,000
Alimony paid (8 mo)	(8,000)
Adjusted income	28,000

For Case B, assume that the wife earns $30,000 in wages, and that the husband is unemployed. They live together four months. The separate maintenance order directs that the wife pay the husband $1,250 as monthly spousal support, until such time as he becomes re-employed. He was unemployed the entire separation year. How are the incomes reported?

In this case, the wife reports as follows—

W-2 wages	30,000
Alimony paid (8 mo)	(10,000)
Adjusted income	20,000

The husband reports—

Earned income	-0-
Alimony received	10,000
Total income	10,000

In both these cases (A and B), you will note that the spousal support is treated as alimony. Nowhere on Form 1040 is there any line identifying an entry as "spousal support." There is one line in the income portion identified as *alimony received*. There is another line in the adjustments portion identified as *alimony paid*. By the position of these lines on Form 1040, it is self-evident that alimony received is income, and that alimony paid is an adjustment to (subtraction from) income.

In the tax code, alimony and spousal support are treated as one and the same. However, instead of using the phrase "spousal support," Sections 71(a) [income] and 215(a) [deduction] use the phrase *separate maintenance payments* interchangeably with the word "alimony." Specifically, Section 71(a) says—

Gross income includes amounts received as alimony or separate maintenance payments.

Then Section 215(a) says—

In the case of an individual, there shall be allowed as a deduction an amount equal to the alimony or separate maintenance payments paid during the taxable year.

5

INNOCENT SPOUSE RELIEF

> The Co-Liability Feature Of A Joint Return Is Suspended, Tentatively Speaking, Under IRC Section 6015. Newly Enacted In 1998, A Tax-Injured Spouse MAY ELECT To Seek Relief. The Key Prerequisite Is An UNDERSTATEMENT OF TAX Caused By One Or More Erroneous Items On A Return By One Or Both Spouses. Understatement Occurs When A Formal "Notice" Of Deficiency Or Collection Liability Is Received. Within 6 Months, Request For Relief From Co-Liability Is Made On Form 8857. If The IRS Does Not Respond, Or Responds Unfavorably, A Petition To The U.S. Tax Court May Be Filed For Judicial Review.

Initiating separate returns after several or more years of joint returns does not exonerate the spouses of their joint and several liabilities for the previous returns. When the marriage becomes disharmonious, as separate returns imply, the spouses tend to clam up regarding items on the prior returns. Consequently, there is always a risk of significant understatement of tax caused by an erroneous item thereon by one spouse or the other. When this happens, the more easily accessible spouse is IRS dunned for the total liability of both.

When a joint return has been filed, and the IRS determines several years later that there is an understatement of tax, the IRS is authorized to go after each spouse individually. The usual practice is to address a Notice of Adjustment or other formal notice to both spouses jointly, at the last joint address. At this point, the IRS does not know that the spouses may be living apart and preparing separate returns. The result often is that the joint notice goes unnoticed or is ignored altogether. The spouse actually receiving the notice may feel that he or she is innocent of the erroneous item, and that somehow the IRS knows this. In the meantime, the spouse causing the erroneous items makes himself/herself inaccessible for collections processing. This leaves the IRS little choice but to go after the innocent spouse.

BUT, if certain conditions are met, the innocent spouse can be relieved of the tax liability caused by the other spouse. This is the essence of **Section 6015** of the IR Code. This section is titled: ***Relief from Joint and Several Liability on Joint Return***. This section also establishes procedures to limit liability for spouses who are no longer married, legally separated, or not living together.

In this chapter, therefore, we want to familiarize you with Section 6015 and address other features affirming the inequity of joint and several liability in particular situations. We caution you, though, that specific conditions must be met based on provable facts and circumstances. Allegations of innocence will not do. Off-the-wall suspicions of wrongdoing by the other spouse are too general to be treated as credible.

Overview of Section 6015

Section 6015 is "new law" in its entirety. It applies to any spousal tax liability arising after July 22, 1998. It also applies to any such liability arising on or before July 22, 1998 remaining unpaid as of that date. The enactment of Section 6015 repealed its "old law" counterpart: Section 6013(e). Said old law was titled: ***Spouse Relieved of Liability in Certain Cases***. Except for its repeal of subsection (e), Section 6013 remains fully intact. Section 6013 is titled: ***Joint Return of Income Tax by Husband and Wife***. By assigning co-liability relief to a stand-alone section of the tax code, Congress is finally coming to grips with a longstanding tax administration problem that just won't go away on its own.

Section 6015 comprises about 3,000 statutory words. This word count is spread over the following six (rather extensive) subsections:

(a) In General: Notwithstanding
(b) Procedures for Relief from Liability Applicable to All Joint Filers
(c) Procedures to Limit Liability for Taxpayers No Longer Married or Taxpayers Legally Separated or Not Living Together
(d) Allocation of Deficiency
(e) Petition for Review by Tax Court
(f) Equitable Relief

As with all tax laws, simplicity and clarity in the subsections of Section 6015 are not their virtues. Any ambiguity — or perceived ambiguity — is an opportunity for the IRS to disallow relief, even though the Congressional intent is reasonably explicit.

In the Committee Reports (on P.L. 105-206) leading up to Section 6015, Congress stated—

The bill generally makes innocent spouse relief easier to obtain. [It] eliminates all of the understatement thresholds and requires only that the understatement of tax be attributable to an erroneous (and not just a grossly erroneous) item of the other spouse. . . . The bill [also] provides that innocent spouse relief may be provided on an apportioned basis. That is, the spouse may be relieved of liability as an innocent spouse to the extent the liability is attributable to the portion of an understatement of tax which the spouse did not know of and had no reason to know of.

This kind of legislative intent is often lost in the statutory words which an innocent spouse must confront. For example, the preamble clause in Section 6015(a) says—

Notwithstanding section 6013(d)(3) . . . may elect to seek relief under the procedures prescribed under subsection (b), and . . . under subsection (c).

Subsection 6013(d)(3) reads—

If a joint return is made, the tax shall be computed on the aggregate income and the liability with respect to the tax shall be joint and several.

In other words, for an innocent spouse seeking tax relief, the joint and several liability which the IRS is empowered to enforce is temporarily set aside. This is the significance of the statutory word: *Notwithstanding*. So, too, are community property laws in those states which enforce their tax collection efforts against an innocent spouse under "community property" theory.

Is There: Understatement of Tax?

Innocent spouse relief is not intended to be a negotiating tool with the other spouse in a divorce proceeding or in circumstances leading up to such a proceeding. First of all, there has to be some bona fide understatement of tax on a joint return. The understatement has to be real and determinable in amount. And at least part of the understatement must be attributable to some erroneous item or items on the return by the other spouse. Innocent oversights and harmless errors do not count. Under emotional stress, either party can cause some error unintentionally.

An "understatement of tax" does not arise until the IRS, in one manner or another, notifies one or both spouses that additional tax is due. At that time, the amount of additional tax — called: *deficiency* — must be evaluated in terms of errors made on the original return (or returns). Typical errors include omissions of income, understatements of income, overstatements of deductions, mis-statements of basis in property, overclaims of exemptions and credits, and arithmetical additions, subtractions, and transfers. Are the errors intentional or inadvertent? Whichever the case, each error should be assigned to the spouse who caused it. Only then can it be argued that one spouse is innocent (or mostly so) and the other is not innocent (and very cunning).

For the purpose of determining if there is an understatement of tax, subsection 6015(b) relies on subsection 6662(d)(2): *Understatement*. Said referenced subsection reads—

> *The term "understatement" means **the excess of**—*
> *(i)   the amount of tax required to be shown . . . , over*
> *(ii)   the amount of tax imposed which is* [already] *shown on the return.*

In other words, the IRS has to examine the joint return and determine that, indeed, a deficiency exists. Until the IRS actually does this, there are no grounds for seeking innocent spouse relief. As a strategy in divorce proceedings, raising an "innocent spouse" issue has no tax standing whatsoever.

How "Innocence" Determined

Section 6015(b): *Relief from* [Joint] *Liability*, requires that—

On such return there is an understatement of tax attributable [entirely] to erroneous items of 1 individual filing the joint return.

This is just one of the essential prerequisites for seeking 100% innocent spouse relief.

An equally important, and perhaps more important, prerequisite is the degree of innocence of the relief-seeking spouse. The statutory words in this regard are—

*The other individual filing the joint return establishes that in signing the return he or she **did not know, and had no reason to know**, there was such understatement.* [Emphasis added.]

Thus, not knowing or having no reason to know is the genesis of what truly defines an innocent spouse. This genesis is called the "knowledge standard" (or "knowledge of understatement" or "knowledge of transaction") in tax policy circles.

The courts have anguished over the knowledge standard for many years before the enactment of Section 6015. The consensus was that any actual or constructive knowledge of the underlying transaction was sufficient to deny relief. In the case of *P.A. Price* [CA-9, 89-2 USTC ¶ 9598, 887 F2d 959], the court took a different tack. It granted relief even though the wife knew that a large deduction for a gold mining venture had been claimed by her husband. She did not know that there was an understatement of tax; she had no involvement in the mining venture; her husband prepared the joint return; and she was misled by her husband.

The *Price* court considered five factors when analyzing the extent of the wife's knowledge of the tax preparation affairs. It considered:

(1)   the spouse's level of education;
(2)   his or her involvement in the family's financial affairs;
(3)   his or her involvement in the other spouse's business affairs (with respect to tax return preparation);
(4)   the presence of unusual or lavish expenditures; and
(5)   the culpable spouse's deceit or evasiveness.

Other courts have considered such factors as: (i) small children to attend to; (ii) expenditures double or triple reported income; (iii) spouse's gambling losses; (iv) abuse and threats of violence; (v) heavy alcoholic consumption; (vi) what a reasonably prudent spouse should question; and (vii) amount of time allowed for reviewing and signing the return. Still and all, the "*Price* standard" is increasingly being used for judicial rulings on the innocence of the relief-seeking spouse. How much did the innocent spouse really know, and did said spouse "tacitly consent" to the other spouse's activities?

In Figure 5.1, we list in abbreviated form the statutory requirements for 100% innocent spouse relief. The essence is that the "other spouse" is solely responsible for the erroneous item or items that gave rise to the tax deficiency.

A Convincing Example

In the past, the IRS has been neither sympathetic nor gracious towards innocent spouses. It maintained a hard line until the bitter end. The end only came after the injured spouse sought relief in the U.S. Tax Court. This meant hiring professional assistance to present the underlying facts to said court. Here's a true case on point in which the author prepared the petition to the Tax Court. Even the IRS was convinced that the relief-seeking spouse was truly innocent. The case was based on the old-law standard of "grossly erroneous."

The petitioner, wife, filed a joint return with her husband for the tax year 1987. The return was not actually signed by either spouse,

IRC Sec. 6015 (b)	PROCEDURES FOR RELIEF FROM LIABILITY APPLICABLE TO ALL JOINT FILERS

A	A joint return for any taxable year.
B	On such return, an understatement of tax attributable to erroneous items by the other spouse.
C	Spouse seeking relief had no knowledge of the understatement when signing the joint return.
D	Inequitable to hold relief seeking spouse liable for tax misdeeds of the other spouse.
E	Relief sought within 2 years after IRS commences collection activities against the relief seeking spouse.

... Then the relief seeking spouse **SHALL BE RELIEVED** of liability for tax (including interest, penalties, and other amounts) to the extent such liability is attributable to the understatement by the other spouse.

Fig. 5.1 - The Requirements for Mandatory 100% Innocent Spouse Relief

but was signed by an authorized agent (in a well-established accounting firm). The husband, a real estate attorney, supplied all of the tax information for the return. He was the principal owner in a series of real estate ventures and development projects. The wife never worked in the business world, though she did work in her husband's legal office as a temporary substitute when some regular clerical staff member was out sick.

After 20 years of marriage, the couple were divorced on April 9, 1990. On September 20, 1991, the wife received a Notice of Deficiency from the IRS for $155,178 (including penalties and interest). (Yes: $155,178 was *the actual figure!*) The deficiency was for the 1987 return, filed late in 1988. The IRS threatened to record a Federal Tax Lien against her home. The wife was horrified and panic stricken. Who wouldn't be?

Nevertheless, here's how the wife pleaded her case to the U.S. Tax Court:

The facts upon which the petitioner relies, as the basis for innocent spouse relief are as follows:

(a) Petitioner is a housewife who participated in no manner whatsoever in the preparation of the joint return for 1987. Petitioner did not personally sign the return, but recalls vaguely signing a power of attorney designating the accounting firm of _____ to act as petitioner's agent.

(b) The alleged $155,178 deficiency on the return derives from a fictitious business known as _____. The principal asset of the "business" (a house) was wholly owned by petitioner's husband and another (female) residential party named_____.
Petitioner's name was not associated with that property in any way.

(c) The female party in (b) above was a long-standing extramarital affair carried on by petitioner's husband. That jointly-owned house was located approximately 600 miles from petitioner's residence. Petitioner had no prior knowledge of this affair whatsoever. It was discovered by petitioner's attorney after the divorce was final.

(d) The substantial understatement results from a disallowed capital loss in the alleged "business" in (b) above, in the amount of $554,205. This amount of capital loss was entered on the joint return by petitioner's husband, without any disclosure to or consultation with the petitioner. The petitioner has always been compelled to sign documents, without the opportunity to read or discuss them. Husband was always in a hurry when directing petitioner to "sign here."

(e) The amount of $554,205 in (d) above is grossly erroneous in that it is without any basis in fact or law. This amount was the cost of a personal residence which was owned jointly by petitioner's husband and the female party named in (b) above. The residence was occupied by both persons extramaritally prior to petitioner's divorce becoming final. As part of the extramarital settlement, the residence was relinquished in 1987 to the female party so named.

(f) With respect to the substantial understatement of tax described above, petitioner has met all of the conditions for statutory relief of liability as set forth in IRC Sec. 6013(e).

WHEREFORE, petitioner prays that she be relieved of all liability for the $155,178 deficiency in tax for 1987.

/s/
_____
Petitioner

Before the case went to trial, the IRS conceded the issue and granted 100% of the relief sought. That's $155,178 in innocent spouse tax relief! Subsequently, the IRS went after the former husband who pleaded no contest. He paid it all.

Now, to Form 8857

Prior to 1998 (enactment of Section 6015), petitioning the Tax Court was the only way to get innocent spouse relief. Now, there is Form 8857: *Request for Innocent Spouse Relief.* Said form must be submitted within two years after being notified by the IRS of an understatement of tax. This form is a much simpler way to go. However, a petition to the Tax Court may still be initiated, if the IRS responds unfavorably to your Form 8857 request. The IRS has six months to respond, and generally does so within such time.

Form 8857 consists of four parts, nine questions, and six Yes-No checkboxes. Part I identifies your spouse or former spouse, then asks:

*Do you have an **Understatement of Tax**?*
☐ *Yes, Go to Part II*
☐ *No, Go to Part IV*

Part II asks if you are divorced, legally separated, or have lived apart . . . *at all times during the 12-month period prior to filing this form.* If you answer "Yes" to any of these questions, you are then instructed:

Check here ▶ ☐ *and go to Part III.*
*You may request **Separation of Liability** (see instructions).*

Part III asks: *Is the understatement of tax due to the **Erroneous Items** of your spouse?*

☐ *Yes. You may request **Innocent Spouse Relief** (see instructions).*

☐ *No. You may request **Equitable Relief** for the understatement of tax. Check **Yes** in Part IV.*

Part IV asks: *Do you have an **Underpayment of Tax** . . . or another tax liability that qualifies for **Equitable Relief?***

☐ *Yes. You may request **Equitable Relief** (see instructions).*

☐ *No. You cannot file this form unless* [you have an understatement of tax].

In Figure 5.2, we summarize the essence of Form 8857. Especially note that one of three types of relief can be sought. For each type sought, you must attach a statement citing the pertinent facts and circumstances as you know them. In the $155,178 relief case above, we illustrated the kinds of facts and circumstances that you should present.

What the Instructions Say

There are three pages of instructions to Form 8857, comprising approximately 2,600 words. These instructions are quite clear . . . surprisingly so. If you are a candidate spouse seeking understatement-of-tax relief, phone the IRS on its *Tax Forms 800#*. Request a copy of the form and its instructions, plus **Publication 971**: *Innocent Spouse Relief.*

The purpose of Form 8857, of course, is to request of the IRS the types of relief indicated in Figure 5.2. In this regard, the instructions say—

> *You must attach a statement to Form 8857 explaining why you qualify for relief. Complete the statement using the best information you have available. Include your name and social security number (SSN) on the statement. . . . If you are requesting relief for more than 1 tax year, you only need to file one Form 8857. However, you must include a **separate***

*statement for each year. . . . The IRS will evaluate your request and tell you if you qualify. . . . If the IRS sends you a **determination notice** denying in whole or in part your request for relief, **or** you do not receive a determination notice within 6 months . . . you may petition the Tax Court to review your case.*

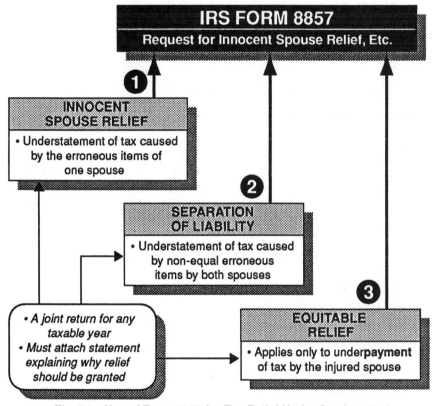

Fig. 5.2 - Use of Form 8857 for Tax Relief Under Section 6015

Form 8857 uses two different qualifying terms which tend to be confusing. The two terms are: **Understatement** of tax and **Underpayment** of tax. What's the difference?

An "under**statement**" of tax (or deficiency) is the difference between the total amount of tax that the IRS determines *should have been shown* on the return, and the amount that was actually shown. For example, a joint return was filed showing a tax of $5,000. This full amount was paid with submission of the return. Later, the IRS determines that the tax should have been $16,500. The understatement amount is $11,500 (16,500 – 5,000).

An "under**payment**" of tax is that amount properly shown on your return, but which has not been fully paid. In the example above, you filed a joint return properly showing $16,500 due. You attached a check for "your share" in the amount of $6,500. Your spouse (or former spouse) was supposed to attach his or her $10,000 check before mailing the return. Your spouse did not attach his/her check, though the return was mailed on time. There is an underpayment of $10,000 for which you and your spouse are both liable.

The instructions on Form 8857 say—

*Note: If you have both an understatement and underpayment of tax, you may have to request different types of relief. You may only request "equitable relief" for the **underpayment** of tax.*

What is "Equitable Relief"?

Section 6015(f) of the IR Code defines *Equitable Relief* as—

If—
(1) taking into account all the facts and circumstances, it is inequitable to hold the individual liable for any unpaid tax or any deficiency (or any portion of either); and

(2) relief is not available to such individual under subsection (b) [innocent spouse relief] *or (c)* [separation of liability],

the [IRS] *may relieve such individual of such liability.*

Incidentally, the general definition of the term "equitable" is that which is characterized by fairness irrespective of law.

Note above that the IRS's equitable relief authority is discretionary: not mandatory. The law says: *may relieve*. It does not say: shall relieve. This is your guarantee that the IRS will grant such relief only in the most unusual of circumstances. We have a real life case to illustrate this point.

The spouses physically separated in 1997 when the husband moved out suddenly and filed for divorce. For that year, each spouse prepared a separate return. The husband's tax liability was $46,792 which he paid. The wife's tax liability was $10,985 which she could not pay. She sought equitable relief from the IRS under the provisions of Section 6015(f). The IRS denied her request, saying that she failed to provide sufficient information. It sent her a deficiency notice for $11,190 (including penalty).

The wife protested. She pointed out in a formal statement (with bank records attached) that the day before the husband left, the joint account balance was $47,683. The day after he moved out, the balance was $1,119. Thus, the husband had taken $46,564 (47,683 − 1,119) of community funds: an uncanny match to the husband's separate tax liability above. This action left the wife destitute.

It took a good six months back and forth between the IRS and the destitute wife (via her tax rep) before the IRS granted full relief in mid-1999. Subsequently, the former husband involuntarily paid the wife's amount. He was court ordered to do so.

Separate Liability Election

The general rule is that once a joint return is filed, the spouses cannot go back and file separate returns. We included this prohibition in Figure 3.4 when filing an amended return. But what happens if a deficiency is assessed by the IRS several years after the spouses are divorced, legally separated, or living totally apart? Particularly, if both spouses contributed to the deficiency to a non-50/50 extent. This is where IRC Section 6015(c): *Election for Separation of Liability*, comes in.

In essence, Section 6015(c) says—

*If an individual who has made a joint return for any taxable year **elects** the application of this subsection, the individual's liability **for any deficiency** which is assessed . . . **shall not** exceed the portion of such deficiency **properly allocable** to the individual.* [Emphasis added.]

The allocation proceeds as if each had filed a married separate return. Each spouse is responsible for his/her own erroneous omissions, understatements, overstatements, and credits that contributed to the deficiency [subsec. 6015(d)]. The election is not valid if there is any evidence of intentional wrongdoing that is known to the electing spouse.

The idea behind the election is the inequity caused by the joint-and-several-liability rule. The allocation principle is the assessed deficiency times the ratio of erroneous items of the electing spouse to the total erroneous items of both spouses. We portray this allocation concept for you in Figure 5.3.

For example, suppose the assessed deficiency on a joint return was $3,864. At a 28% effective tax rate, the $3,864 deficiency equates to $13,800 of erroneous items by both spouses [3,864 ÷ 0.28]. Of this $13,800 of erroneous items, suppose $3,800 is attributable to the electing spouse (the wife). In this case, the wife's share of the jointly assessed liability would be

$$\$3,864 \text{ deficiency} \times \frac{3,800 \text{ wife's erroneous items}}{13,800 \text{ total erroneous items}}$$

$$= \$3,864 \times 0.2753 = \underline{\$1,064}$$

Correspondingly, the husband would be responsible for $2,800 [3,864 − 1,064]. After establishing said separate liability, each spouse is responsible for all associated penalties and interest. The relief-seeking spouse establishes the proportionate share.

Recap of Options

The joint-and-several-liability rule has always been an inequity of law concerning truly innocent spouses. The results have been particularly harsh — even devastating — in divorce-related situations. Typically, whichever spouse was the most readily accessible had to endure the full brunt of the often draconian IRS collections actions: levies, liens, seizures, etc. Horror stories abound on the financial and emotional destruction caused by the

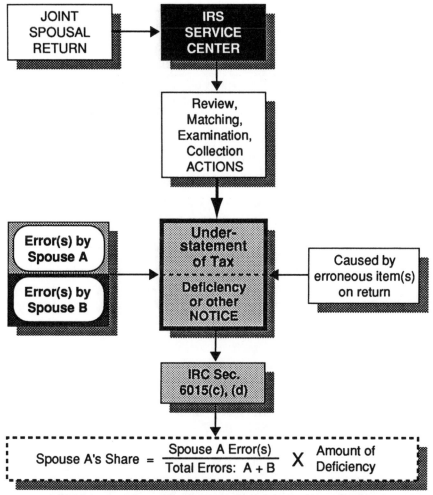

Fig. 5.3 - The Allocable Relief Concept: Separation of Liability

IRS. Code Section 6015 is intended to alleviate the problems of the past. Whether it does so satisfactorily or not remains to be seen.

In late 1999, the IRS published its revised Form 8857: *Request for Innocent Spouse Relief.* The use of this form is now required *before* any court action can be taken by the injured spouse. As previously mentioned, this form permits three different types of elections, namely:

A — Innocent Spouse Relief [Sec. 6015(b)]
B — Separation of Liability [Sec. 6015(c)]
C — Equitable Relief   [Sec. 6015(f)]

In all three elections there must be an attachment to Form 8857 explaining very specifically why relief should be granted. In addition, the instructions say—

Do not file Form 8857 with your tax return or fax it to the IRS. Instead, IF . . .

1. *You are meeting with an IRS employee for an examination, examination appeal, or collection . . . file Form 8857 with that person.*

2. *You received an IRS notice of deficiency, and the 90-day period specified in the notice has not expired . . . file Form 8857 with the IRS employee named in the notice. Attach a copy of the notice of deficiency.* ***Do not*** *file Form 8857 with the Tax Court.*

If neither situation above applies to you, file Form 8857 with—

Internal Revenue Service Center
Cincinnati, OH 45999-0857

Overall, Form 8857 is your best opportunity for getting your tax injuries "on the record." If you are experiencing the likelihood of divorce, or are currently going through such, by all means acquire and acquaint yourself with Form 8857. Then file it with the IRS before your spouse or former spouse does so. Make sure you have in place all relevant facts and documents. As best you can, specify which items on your return are erroneous. Indicate those which are yours, if any, and those which are your spouse's. If you get a favorable response from the IRS, use the response plus your copy of Form 8857 as evidence to support your tax-injured position in the divorce proceedings.

6

CHILD DEPENDENCY

When Financial Support By One Parent Exceeds 50% Of A Child's Total Support, That Parent Gets A $3,000 Dependency Exemption. When One Parent Has Physical Custody Of A Child More Than Six Months, And Furnishes More Than 50% Of The Child's Household Support, That Parent Becomes The Custodial Parent Who May File As "Head Of Household." As Such, The Custodial Parent Gets A 10% Lower Tax Rate Than If Single. Confusion And Controversy Arise Over Dependency Exemption And Head Of Household Status. Because So, Child Support And Custody Arrangements Must Be Clarified In The Decree.

When a marriage has produced one or more children, each spouse's (separate) tax return is affected. The effects are in addition to those matters discussed in the preceding chapters.

The primary effects pertain to child support and child custody. "Support" pertains to financial care and welfare, whereas "custody" pertains to physical housing and guidance. Where there is only one child, one parent may support the child financially while the other parent may house the child physically. Where there is more than one child, the same support-custody division may prevail, or there may be a mixture of both. An understanding of the distinction between parental roles of support and custody is the fundamental key for clarifying the tax effects of the children. Often, the custodial parent wants both benefits: dependency exemption *and* head of household status. This causes much parental controversy.

The Dependency Exemption

The parent who pays more than 50% of the total support of a child gets a $3,000 exemption allowance for that child. If there is more than one child, there is a separate $3,000 exemption for each child. The term "exemption" means that the claiming parent's *taxable income* is reduced by $3,000 for each dependent child.

> *Editorial Note*: The exemption amount per dependent changes from year to year. New legislation and inflation indexing account for this. Adjustments each year make our discussion in this chapter extremely awkward. To avoid the confusion and complexity, we will use $3,000 as a fixed amount. You are cautioned, however, to consult official IRS instructions for the exact figure that is applicable to the particular tax year of your concern.

The exemption allowance is prescribed by Section 151(c) of the tax code, which is titled: *Additional Exemption for Dependents*. In pertinent part it reads (slightly edited) as follows—

An exemption of the exemption amount [$3,000] . . . [shall be allowed] for each dependent . . . who is a child of the taxpayer and who (i) has not attained the age of 19 . . . or (ii) is a student who has not attained the age of 24 . . . at the close of [the] calendar year.

(We will define shortly the terms: "child of the taxpayer" and "student.")

The $3,000 exemption applies also to dependents other than children of the taxpayer. It applies to dependent brothers, sisters, fathers, mothers, relatives, and nonrelatives. But our discussion here is limited strictly to children of divorcing/divorced parents.

The $3,000 exemption for each dependent child is an all-or-nothing affair. It cannot be allocated between the two parents in proportion to the support provided by each. For example, if one parent pays 65% of a child's total support, that parent gets the full $3,000 exemption allowance. There is no 65/35 split whereby one parent gets a $1,950 exemption and the other gets a $1,050 exemption. Only one parent or the other gets the full exemption.

There may be cases where neither parent pays more than 50% of a child's total support. When this happens, neither parent gets the $3,000 allowance. There could be "third party" contributions to a child's support, such as Social Security, public assistance, grandparents, beneficial trusts, military allotments, and so on.

Ordinarily, the more-than-50%-support test applies to an entire tax year. That is, 12 full calendar months: January through December. But if a child is born in August, say, the 50% test applies to only four months of the birth year. If a child dies in June, say, the 50% test applies to six months of the death year. In other words, for the year of birth or year of death of a child, the dependency test applies only to the actual months of life of the child.

For each dependent child, there is only one $3,000 exemption allowance. There are no additional exemptions for handicapped children, blind children, or for other physical or mental impairments. If a parent qualifies for the dependency exemption of a child, he/she is automatically allowed any applicable deductions for medical expenses and care services paid for that child.

Dependent Child Defined

Recall in Section 151(c) above that the phrase "child of the taxpayer" is used. The "taxpayer," of course, is the parent who files his or her own return, and claims a dependent child thereon. The term "child" is defined in Section 151(c)(3) as—

An individual who (within the meaning of section 152) is a son, stepson, daughter, or stepdaughter of the taxpayer.

This definition is primarily directed at the divorcing/divorced parents' natural children. But note the cross-reference to Section 152. Said section: *Dependent Defined*, consists of 26 paragraphs. Only a few are relevant to children as dependents.

One such subsection is 152(b)(2). It broadens the definition of "child" to include a legally adopted child, a child placed in the taxpayer's home by an authorized agency, and a foster child who is a member of the taxpayer's household for the entire taxable year. The key phrase of this subsection is that such a child . . . *shall be treated as a child of such individual by blood*: that is, no differently from a natural child (if the proper qualifications are met).

Ordinarily, a child can be claimed as a dependent for the $3,000 exemption only if he or she has not attained the age of 19. This is spelled out quite clearly in subsection 151(c)(1)(B), namely—

> *A child of the taxpayer who has not attained the age of 19 at the close of the calendar year in which the taxable year of the taxpayer begins.*

Thus — technically — the year in which a child becomes age 19 is not a dependency year. Many parents will question this.

There is one clearly defined statutory exception to the age 19 limitation. A "student" (child) can be any age up to 24 and still be claimed as a dependent. As per subsection 151(c)(4), the term "student" means—

> *An individual who during each of 5 calendar months during the . . . taxable year of the taxpayer . . . is a full-time student at an educational organization . . . or, is pursuing a full-time course of institutional on-farm training.*

A *full-time student* is one enrolled for the number of hours or courses considered full-time attendance at a "recognized" school or college. The school or college must be an educational institution with a regular faculty, an established curriculum, with an organized body of students attending. Its "credits" are recognized by, and transferable to, other schools. Night schools, correspondence schools, employer training courses, hospital internships, handicap centers, and the like, do not qualify as full-time student educational organizations.

If Over Age 19

What if a child is not a full-time student, is over age 19, is not regularly employed, and lives at home with one of his parents? Is he (or she) to be kicked out on the street? Could not a parent claim such a child as a dependent, and take the $3,000 exemption?

Yes, one parent can.

The primary purpose of the not-attained-age-19 feature is to make federal law on child support more compatible with state laws on age of majority. The age of majority in most states ranges from 16 to 19. Up to this age, state laws can compel a parent to support his/her child (or children). After the age of majority, state compulsion does not apply. But we all know that many parents support their children well past the age of majority. They do this as concerned humanitarians where a child cannot become self-supportive the moment he/she attains age 19.

A child who is no longer a minor under state law can still be claimed as a dependent under the general rule of Section 152(a): *General Definition*. This rule says in part that—

The term "dependent" means any of the following individuals over half of whose support, for the calendar year in which the taxable year of the taxpayer begins, was received from the taxpayer (or is treated . . . as received):
(1)   a son or daughter of the taxpayer,
(3)   a stepson or stepdaughter of the taxpayer.
. . . and so on.

So, regardless of a child's age, if one parent or the other pays "over half" of the child's total support, the dependency exemption can be claimed. This even includes a married child, if such child does not file a joint return with his (or her) spouse.

"Total Support" Defined

The exact statutory phrase (Section 152(a)) qualifying a parent for a child exemption is—

. . . over half of whose support, for the calendar year . . . was received from the taxpayer.

Every divorced or separated parent claiming a child as a dependent should memorize this phrase. It is easier to memorize a federal tax phrase if its words are translated into everyday language.

The "over half" means *more than 50%*; "whose support" means *total support*; "calendar year" means *each year separately*; and "received from" means *paid by* . . . in each calendar year. Most parents understand what more than 50% means, but they do not understand the concept of "total support." Just what does the term "support" include?

Authoritative guidance on this issue can be found in Regulation 1.152-1(a)(2)(i): *General definition of a dependent.* This particular regulation is crucial to our presentation here. It reads in full as follows:

> *For purposes of determining whether or not an individual received, for a given calendar year, over half of his support from the taxpayer, there shall be taken into account the amount of support received from the taxpayer as compared to the entire amount of support which the individual received from all sources, including support which the individual himself supplied. The term "support" includes food, shelter, clothing, medical and dental care, education, and the like. Generally, the amount of an item of support will be the amount of expense incurred by the one furnishing such item. If the item of support furnished an individual is in the form of property or lodging, it will be necessary to measure the amount of such item of support in terms of its fair market value.*

This regulation is really not as complicated as it may appear upon a first quick reading. It actually makes good sense. So, please, go back and read it again.

Particularly note the phrase "item of support." An item of support is *any expenditure* actually made for the support, rearing, and development of a child into responsible adulthood. It includes such sundry items as grooming supplies, vacation trips, sport gear and sporting events, gifts of all kinds (if used by the child), special courses and classes, transportation needs, wedding expenses, and so on. In other words, total support encompasses all expenses for a child which are not clearly extravagant or illegal. For example, giving a child a sport car capable of 120 miles per hour speed, obviously would not be classed as an item of support. There is no standard support amount in X-dollars per month. Much depends on the financial capability of those providing the support. The support may be provided by one individual . . . or by five individuals.

Illustrative Example

Total support not only means all expenses, it also means those incurred by *all sources*. Any one and everyone contributing to a child's support is counted. This includes contributions, if any, by the dependent himself.

This "all source" concept is quite clearly stated in Regulation 1.152-1(a)(2)(i) cited above. That is—

> . . . *the entire amount of support which the individual receives from all sources, including support which the individual himself supplied.*

In most cases, both parents contribute — usually unequally — to the support of their child. In addition, it is also quite common for a "third parent" to contribute. A third parent may be a step-parent (where one of the natural parents remarries), a foster parent, a grandparent, or a godparent (such as an uncle, aunt, close friend). In some cases, the child himself may contribute partially to his own support from part-time earnings, savings, or insurance proceeds. Thus, total support is not a one-parent-only endeavor; it is a supportive arrangement by multiple sources.

Where there are multiple sources, each item of support by each contributor must be clearly identified and noted. He who pays more than 50% of the total support (for a given year) gets the dependency exemption. Let us illustrate the situation with a typical example.

Consider that a father, mother, and grandparent contribute to a child's support. The child lives with his mother. He draws $350 from his savings which he spends on himself. The father is under court order to pay $200 per month, which is spent by the mother mostly for food, clothing, and medical expenses for the child. The father also pays additional amounts which he can substantiate. The mother contributes mostly the household expenses, such as furnishings, utilities, and maintenance. The grandparent contributes mostly towards vacations and sporting events. Assume that the total expenditures for support of the child are $5,000 for the year, and that the amount provided by each individual is documented.

If push comes to shove (between father and mother), a carefully itemized support record would have to be prepared. For illustrative purposes, this is done in Figure 6.1. We urge you to study Figure 6.1 carefully. It represents a lot of tax wisdom. Particularly note the detailed listing of items of support. We show 15 such items. When there is controversy between parents, the most practical way to resolve the matter is a listing such as Figure 6.1.

	ITEM OF SUPPORT	Paid by FATHER	Paid by MOTHER	Paid by GRAND PARENT	Paid by CHILD	TOTALS
1.	Food	1,200				1,200
2.	Clothing	250			100	350
3.	Grooming	75		100		175
4.	Medical	300				300
5.	Education	250				250
6.	Shelter	300	600			900
7.	Furnishings		75			75
8.	Utilities		150			150
9.	Maintenance		50	100		150
10.	Insurance		75			75
11.	Transportation	100		100		200
12.	Recreation	150			150	300
13.	Vacation			300		300
14.	Church		100			100
15.	Other	100	75	200	100	475
	TOTALS	$ 2,725	$ 1,125	$ 800	$ 350	$ 5,000
	PERCENTAGES	54.5%	22.5%	16.0%	7.0%	100%

Fig. 6.1 - Illustrative Itemization: Support for a Dependent Child

Figure 6.1 illustrates several important points, namely:

One. The number of items of support is not limited to any fixed items. Whatever is actually spent counts.

Two. The amounts paid by each contributor are allocated to specific items of support.

Three. Of the $5,000 total support, the father contributed $2,725. This is 54.5% which is clearly "over half."

Four. The father was court-required to contribute $2,400. He contributed $325 additionally, for which he gets allocation credit.

Five. The mother contributed $950 towards household expenses for the child, whereas the father contributed only $300. The mother, therefore, can claim "head of household."

If the father had paid no more than the $2,400 court ordered, his share of the total support would have been 48% ($2,400 ÷ $5,000). Would he then get the dependency exemption for the child?

Answer: Yes, he could . . . if.

There is a special rule on this point. If an agreement is signed by all parties concerned, then any party which contributes more than 10% of the total support of a dependent may claim the exemption. Form 2120: *Multiple Support Declaration*, is available for this very purpose.

Maintaining a Household

As we saw in Chapter 3, head of household status is a very important tax option for divorcing and separated parents. To claim this status, one must maintain a household. This "maintaining" requirement is emphasized in Section 2(b): *Definition of Head of Household.* In relevant part it states that—

An individual shall be considered as head of household if, and only if, such individual is not married at the close of his taxable year, . . . and . . . maintains as his home a household which constitutes for more than one-half of such taxable year the principal place of abode, as a member of such household . . . of a son, stepson, daughter, or stepdaughter of the taxpayer.

Regulation 1.2-2(d) goes on to explain what constitutes maintaining a household. In essence, it means paying more than 50% of the cost thereof. In specifics, the regulation states—

A taxpayer shall be considered as maintaining a household only if he pays more than one-half the cost thereof for his taxable year. The cost of maintaining a household shall be the expenses incurred for the mutual benefit of the occupants thereof. . . . The expenses of maintaining a household include property taxes, mortgage interest, rent, utility charges, upkeep and repairs, property insurance, and food consumed on the premises. Such expenses do not include the cost of clothing, education, medical treatment, vacations, life insurance, and transportation . . . [nor] the value of services rendered in the household by the taxpayer or by a person qualifying the taxpayer as head of household.

There are tax accounting problems in maintaining a household. For obvious practical reasons, the expenses are not separated and proportioned to each occupant in accordance with age, sex, and use. Mortgage payments and rent, for example, are not split up and allocated to each occupant. The same is true of utility charges, insurance, maintenance and repairs, and so on. So, how is this accounting difficulty overcome?

Answer: One simply lists all expenses for the entire household (actually paid by the claiming parent), then divides by the number of occupants. If the total household expenses were $3,750, say, and there were three occupants (mother and two children), the portion of those expenses allocated to each occupant would be $1,250 ($3,750 ÷ 3). As a consequence, each separately itemized expense would be divided by three.

As by now should be evident, both total support and household support involve a more-than-50% test. Often, this creates confusion and conflict about which is which and who gets what.

Total support means everything to support a child from all sources, whereas household support means maintaining a domicile only. These two concepts are separable from each other. Being so, they permit divorcing/divorced parents to mutually share in the growth process of their child or children. A schematic representation of these two concepts is presented in Figure 6.2.

The parent maintaining a household for one or more children is called the *custodial parent*. If a child actually resides in a household

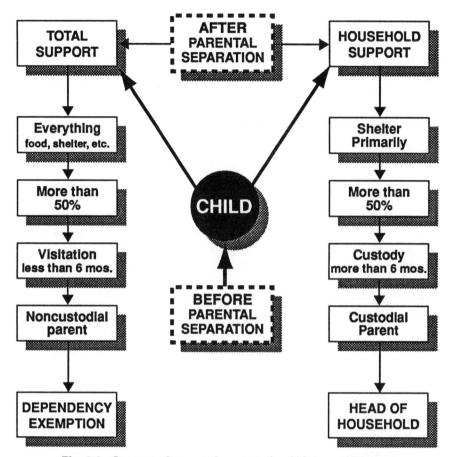

Fig. 6.2 - Separate Support Concepts for Children of Divorce

(including temporary absences while at school) more than six months of the year, it is presumed that the custodial parent actually paid more than 50% of the household expenses. This presumption is not often contested, provided the custodial parent sticks to household support. Any attempt to improperly expand household support into total support will inevitably create tax conflict between the parents involved. Avoiding unnecessary parental conflict is what Figure 6.2 is all about.

It is very important to understand the distinction between total support and household support. The parent paying more than 50% of the total support of the child gets a dependency exemption of

$3,000. This is usually the noncustodial parent: more often than not, the father. If there is more than one child, the noncustodial parent gets $3,000 for *each* child. Such a parent can file a separate tax return as "single plus 1 dependent" (or more, as appropriate).

The parent paying more than 50% of the household support for a child gets "head of household" status. This is a 10% lower tax rate than single status for the same taxable income. This is the custodial parent: more often than not, the mother. If there is more than one child in the household, there is no additional 10% lower tax rate. Head of household is a one-status-only affair, regardless of the number of children involved.

A tax counselor can explain the above distinctions to concerned parents until he is blue in the face. The noncustodial parent would probably understand, but the custodial parent would not (probably). Almost invariably, the custodial parent will claim head of household status *plus* a $3,000 exemption for each child in the household. That is, the custodial parent wants it both ways.

Child support payments made to the custodial parent are not taxable income to that parent. It is tax-free money, pure and straight. Consequently, such parent feels that when she spends the money on the child (or children), she should be entitled to claim it as her contribution to the child's total support. Besides, how can the noncustodial parent establish otherwise? He does not know what is actually paid out for each child's support. Under these circumstances, the noncustodial parent is left "dangling" in his efforts to prove his entitlement to a dependency exemption for each child. The dangling is made worse if the noncustodial parent fails to make his support payments on time, or pays insufficient amounts.

Custodial Parent Presumption

Under federal tax law, dangling cases are resolved in favor of the custodial parent. That is, it is *presumed* that the parent having custody for the greater portion of the year is treated as having paid more than half of a child's total support for that year.

The specific Internal Revenue Code citation is Section 152(e)(1). This section is titled: ***Support Test in Case of Child of Divorced Parents, Etc.; Custodial parent gets exemption.*** As you will see below, the "Etc." includes parents who are going through divorce and who are living apart under various arrangements. The focus is on the relative custodial care by two parents only.

The statutory wording on point is as follows:

> *Except as otherwise provided . . ., if—*
> *(A) a child . . . receives over half of his support during the calendar year from his parents—*
> > *(i) who are . . . legally separated under a decree of . . . separate maintenance,*
> > *(ii) who are separated under a written separation agreement, or*
> > *(iii) who live apart at all times during the last 6 months of the calendar year, and*
> *(B) such child is in the custody of one or both parents for more than one-half of the calendar year,*
> *such child shall be treated . . . as receiving over half of his support . . . from the parent having custody for a greater portion of the calendar year.*

Let's put this wording into a clearer perspective. To do so, suppose the child was in the custody of his father for three months; in the custody of his mother for four months; and in the custody of his grandparents for five months. During each period, the child is fully supported by the custodial person. Who gets the dependency exemption?

Answer: The mother.

During seven months of the year, both parents paid more than half of the child's total support. Also, the child was in the custody of both parents more than half of the year (seven months). The *parent* having custody the greater portion of the year (four months in this case) gets the $3,000 dependency exemption. The same parent also gets head of household status!

Release of Claim to Exemption

The opening phrase in Section 152(e)(1) is: *Except as otherwise provided.* This is your clue that the statutory presumption can be overridden. There is an exception. To take advantage of this exception, a written declaration is required.

The statutory provision for the exception is Section 152(e)(2). This subsection carries the official heading: *Exception where custodial parent releases claim to exemption for the year.* This heading almost is a sentence in itself, which tells all. The exception applies only to the dependency exemption: *not* to the head of household status. Head of household status is more a factual determination based on where the child actually stayed . . . and on how long during the year.

Again, we want to point out, as we did in Figure 6.2, that there is understandable confusion over the "support test" for the dependency exemption and head of household status. Both apply the term "over half" to total support and to maintaining a household.

The specific wording of Section 152(e)(2) goes as follows—

*A child of parents . . . shall be treated as having received over half of his support during a calendar year from the **noncustodial parent** if—*
(A) the custodial parent signs a written declaration . . . that such custodial parent will not claim such child as a dependent for . . . such calendar year, and
(B) the noncustodial parent attaches such written declaration to the noncustodial parent's return for the [applicable] *taxable year.* [Emphasis added.]

In the above wording, we purposely omitted the phrase: *in such manner and form as the* [IRS] *may by regulations prescribe.* This phrase means that an official IRS form is prescribed for claiming the child dependency exemption. This is Form 8332: *Release of Claim to Exemption for Child of Divorced or Separated Parents.* An edited arrangement is presented in Figure 6.3.

The Figure 6.3 form (or similar statement) has to be signed by the custodial parent. The form or statement has to be signed each year that the dependency exemption is released. Instructions on the form permit release for the current year only, for a specified number of years, or for all future years. The release year or years is at the sole discretion of the custodial parent.

FORM 8332	RELEASE OF CLAIM TO EXEMPTION FOR CHILD	Tax Year

For Divorced or Separated Parents Only

Attach (each year) to tax return of noncustodial parent

Release of Claim by Custodial Parent

I agree not to claim an exemption for

_____
(name of child or names of children)

Part I . . . .   for current calendar year ___(specify)___

Part II . . . .   for future tax year(s) ___(specify)___

Name & Signature of Custodial Parent	Social Security No.	Date

Fig. 6.3 - Edited Contents/Format of Form 8332

Difficulties with Form 8332

We do urge you to read through the features of Figure 6.3. (Or, better yet, get hold of the official form.) As you do, chances are you may sense difficulties ahead.

The burden is on the noncustodial parent to procure Form 8332 and present it to the custodial parent for signature. Then, the noncustodial parent has to retrieve the signed form. He/she has to do this in sufficient time to attach it to his/her income tax return for the calendar year. This has to be done each year (for each child) that is being financially supported by the noncustodial parent.

Section 152(e)(2) was written with the idea in mind that separated parents with a child (or children) would cooperate. They would do this at least on those tax matters where each parent benefits. The custodial parent gets the child support payment tax free; the noncustodial parent gets a $3,000 per child tax exemption. This presumes, of course, that the noncustodial parent makes the support payments on time, and in full amounts.

But suppose the custodial parent refuses to sign Form 8332, or signs too late for the noncustodial parent to file it on time. If all child support payments are made, should the noncustodial parent give up (and have his return held hostage by the custodial parent)?

Absolutely not!

Our suggestion is this. The noncustodial parent should fill out Form 8332 in all the proper places. Mark with a red "X" the blank space for the custodial parent's signature. Send the form, with a request for signature, by Certified Mail (with return receipt). Send it before March 15 so as to allow a reasonable 30 days for reply. Remind that person that you are seeking only the dependency exemption: not the head of household status.

If no reply within 30 days, go ahead and claim the child dependency exemption(s) on your tax return. Attach a photocopy of the filled-out Form 8332 showing the red "X" blank space. Attach also a photocopy of your certified mail receipt and your request-for-signature instructions. In addition, photocopy all of your canceled checks for child support payments and attach to the unsigned Form 8332. Then get prepared to thrash the matter out later with the IRS. The tax presumption is on the custodial parent's side. It is a "presumption" only. With good records along the lines of Figure 6.1, the parent claiming the dependency exemption should prevail.

Form 2038 Questionnaire

Most parents have strong emotional principles concerning their children. As a result, sooner or later, one parent is going to overclaim his (or her) dependency exemptions. When this happens, there will be duplicate exemptions for the same child. For obvious tax reasons, duplicate exemptions cannot be allowed. So, what does the IRS do about this?

Sooner or later, the Computer picks up the overclaim and/or duplicate exemption. Then the IRS sends out a form questionnaire to both parents. It is Form 2038 titled: *Questionnaire — Exemption Claimed for Dependent*. A separate form is sent for each child named on a 1040 return, for each year the child's name appears. If there were three children, say, listed three years in a row, that would be nine questionnaires sent to the father *and* nine questionnaires sent to the mother.

The leadoff wording on Form 2038 states:

The information requested on this questionnaire is needed to support the exemption for a dependent claimed on your Federal income tax return. Please complete this form by giving information about the dependent named above. The attached information guide contains tests for claiming dependents and other helpful instructions.

There are 34 question blocks on Form 2038. Many have subquestions thereunder. It is a very comprehensive questionnaire indeed. For example, Question 14 actually has five subquestions. The lead question is:

Were you and the child's other parent divorced, legally separated, or separated under a written separation agreement for any part of the year shown above?

☐ *Yes*   ☐ *No*

If "Yes," there are other subquestions to answer concerning child support and custody arrangements. If "No," then the marital status is questioned. The answering parent must show the dollar amount contributed by the other parent for the child's support.
Tax questionnaires can take time, and if not answered promptly (usually within 15 days), can result in all dependency exemptions being disallowed arbitrarily. If only one parent responds, the other's claim will be disallowed. If both parents respond, and there is a duplication of claims, audit will ensue. Tax audits also take time; they get into other spousal contrary issues, and may ultimately result in the dependency exemptions being disallowed on both parents' returns.

Separate Child Support Order

Because each parent gets some tax benefit, albeit modest, it behooves the parents to resolve their conflicts over child dependency issues well ahead of time. If the parents are civil and cooperative, the resolution can be achieved by an informal child support agreement. Such agreement could be prepared by the parents themselves, or by a nonattorney. Otherwise, attorneys (his and hers) will be needed to prepare a formal Child Support Order. Hopefully, the order would be forthright and clear.

Back in Chapter 2, particularly in Figure 2.5 on page 2-20, we tried to set the sequence for a child support order. We showed it as immediately following a separate (spousal) maintenance order. Actually, both orders could be prepared and presented at the same court hearing. But, for tax reasons, the two orders must be separate documents and completely detachable from each other. All too frequently, attorneys tend to shrug off tax matters in which they are not likely to be involved (such as when the IRS gets into the act). Also, they tend to mix things up. You can't tell which items are spousal support and which are child support. Spousal support enables the payer to get a tax deduction for the entire amount paid. Child support limits the payer to a $3,000 tax exemption for each dependent child, regardless of the amount actually paid. Two different sets of tax rules are involved. Hence, there should be two different legal documents.

There is no reason why a child support order could not be prepared as a self-contained document of its own, devoid of spousal support matters and property settlement terms. If prepared with the assistance of an attorney, it will satisfy state law by showing the signature/name thereon of a superior court judge. This would make it an enforceable legal document against both parents: custodial and noncustodial.

The order could also include a statement that if all child support payments in the amount of $_____ per month were made within the taxable year, the payer (noncustodial) parent would be entitled to claim the child dependency exemption on his or her tax return. If the right tax words were used, such as: *release of claim to exemption* (by the custodial parent), the IRS would accept such an order as a substitute Form 8332.

7

ALIMONY PAYMENTS

Alimony Invokes Tax Rules Distinct From Those Applicable To Child Support And Custody Arrangements. This Necessitates A Separate Written Instrument Designating Clearly All Alimony Terms. The Tax Rules Require That Alimony Payments Be Made In Cash (Via Personal Check) From Sources Of Income Taxable To The Payer. For This, The Payer Gets A Deduction From Gross Income. The Amount And Duration Of Payments Must Be Specified In An Instrument "Incident To Divorce." If Payments Decrease By More Than $15,000 From One Year To The Next, Front-Loading Recomputation Rules Apply.

In every divorce situation, there are *two* settlements. They are alimony settlement and property settlement. Each is for an entirely different reason. (Child support is not a "settlement" issue, as both spouses always will remain parents.)

Alimony involves a payment schedule for an ongoing period of time. In contrast, property settlement is a one-time distribution effort. Consequently, the settlement terms must be separate and distinct from each other. Each settlement establishes a completely different tax world of its own.

The key characteristic of alimony (also called: *spousal support*) is that the payment terms are fixed in specific periodic amounts. Except for stated contingencies, the payments become a formal legal obligation that can go on and on. The terms are unlike child support, which involves parental rights and obligations until a child becomes of age and/or is self-supporting.

Alimony is not exactly the same as spousal support. There is a timing difference. Whereas spousal support is a preparatory arrangement pending the final decree of divorce, alimony is an ongoing arrangement *after* the decree.

Only Cash Payments Count

When an alimony settlement has been reached, the spouses become known as "payer" and "payee." The payer is the one making the alimony payments; the payee is the one receiving the payments. These terms also impose a tax obligation on the part of both spouses. The payer gets a tax deduction; the payee gets a tax inclusion. This is called the *deduction-inclusion* concept.

For many years, alimony was deductible by the payer so long as there were "periodic payments, whether or not at regular intervals." This prior tax rule enabled the payer (former spouse) to make all kinds of substitute arrangements, other than cash. For example, transfers of services or property items (including debt instruments of a third party and annuity contracts), executing of debt instruments by payer (on behalf of payee), and payee use of property owned by the payer (where payer paid mortgage installments, property taxes, and insurance premiums) counted as alimony.

With these substitute arrangements, the payer had a tax advantage. He (or she) maintained the source records and could designate what portions were for alimony. The payee (receiver) had no way of knowing how much was for alimony and how much was for other obligations of the payer. More often than not, the payer "stuck" the payee with whatever the payer considered to be alimony. This caused inconsistencies between what the payer deducted on his tax return, and what the payee included on her tax return. Can you imagine the IRS's computer problems in cross-matching the two former spouses' returns?

Commencing in 1985, all alimony payments must be made in *cash* (period)! No substitutes; no in lieu arrangements; no noncash property transfers are allowed. The term "cash" means green paper dollars, personal checks, money orders, electronic transfers, and other traceable transactions. The whole idea is that cash payments can be more easily computer matched by the IRS.

The tax law requiring alimony payments to be in cash is found in Section 71 of the Internal Revenue Code. Section 71 is titled: *Alimony and Separate Maintenance Payments*. The preamble portion of subsection 71(b) states very clearly that—

> *The term "alimony or separate maintenance payment" means any payment in cash if—* [Emphasis added.]

The "if" is followed by several paragraphs of definitizing features. We will cover these features as we proceed below.

The cash-only concept is also embodied in Section 215: *Alimony, Etc., Payments*. Subsection 215(b) states that—

> *The term "alimony . . . payment" means any alimony . . . payment (as defined in section 71(b)).*

Subsection 215(a) also states—

> *In the case of an individual, there shall be allowed as a deduction an amount equal to the alimony or separate maintenance payments paid during such individual's taxable year . . . which is includible in the gross income of the recipient under section 71(a)* [General Rule].

What we are trying to tell you here is that there are two sets of alimony rules in the tax code: Sections 71 and 215. They cross-reference each other. Section 71 focuses primarily on the payee spouse, whereas Section 215 focuses on the payer spouse. The cross-referencing of these two sections is your cue that the computer will demand consistency of the alimony amounts on both the payer and payee returns. This cross-matching is an easy computer task, due to the particular placement of the payer-payee amounts on each of two separate Forms 1040.

As a footnote to the above, the actual "alimony" phrase used in Sections 71 and 215 is: *alimony or separate maintenance payment*. This confirms what we said in Chapter 4 about spousal support (separate maintenance) being treated as alimony on each spouse's separate return.

How Deducted/Included

For tax purposes, the payer has the primary responsibility for documenting the correct amount of cash payments made during the year. A payer's "best evidence" consists of canceled personal checks. If a check is made out properly to the payee (in full name), and goes through the normal processing channels, and is canceled, the cancellation marks and stamps are proof of receipt by the payee. There is no equivocation. The payer paid a specific amount; the payee received the same amount. The cancellation marks and stamps are third-party originations, not subject to payer/payee manipulations.

The authority for tax deducting the amount paid is Section 215(a), previously cited. In that citation, particularly note the word "individual." This clearly applies to *either* husband (former husband) or wife (former wife). It also clearly eliminates payments from nonhuman entities such as trusts, corporations, brokerage firms, credit-card institutions, and the like. Use of the word "individual" reinforces the personal (cash) payment/receipt concept of deductible/includible alimony. It is a good idea to always mark each payment check with the word *alimony* clearly thereon.

In addition to a canceled-check type of documentation, the payer must obtain, and the payee must supply, the payee's social security number. This is directed by Section 215(c): *Requirement of Identification Number.* In pertinent part, this section reads

(1)   Any individual receiving alimony . . . payments is required to furnish such individual's taxpayer identification number to the individual making such payments, and
(2)   the individual making such payments is required to include such taxpayer identification on such individual's return for the taxable year in which such payments are made.

The tax forms 1040 are designed with special lines designated as "Alimony paid" and "Alimony received." The relative placement of these lines on Form 1040 is presented in Figure 7.1. Note that the payer gets a deduction *from* gross income, whereas the payee gets an inclusion *in* gross income. When cross-matching these amounts by IRS computer, if the difference is more than $15,000, a "red flag" goes up.

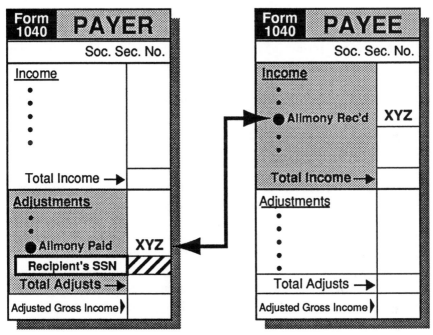

Fig. 7.1 - Cross-Matching of Alimony Amounts on Forms 1040

What Qualifies as "Alimony"

Not all payments between spouses and former spouses qualify as alimony. This is so, even if the parties themselves agree to make their deductions/inclusions computer correct. Only certain payments qualify. Otherwise, cooperative parties could engage in "tax shifting" from year to year, to reduce the total tax from the two returns. Such shifting, if substantial in amount, can cause the IRS to assess penalties.

There are three general qualifications that we want you to know about. First, alimony consists only of those payments made *after* a final decree of divorce has been issued. Such payments are for the settlement of marital rights. These rights are not totally severed until a final judgment on dissolution of the marriage is decreed. At this point, the parties are restored legally to unmarried status.

The second general qualifying requirement is that alimony must be a specific (fixed) payment amount. The amount may be expressed in dollars, or in a percentage of a specifically identified source of income that can be converted to dollars. The amounts may be payable monthly, quarterly, or annually. They must be payable at least once a year. This requirement puts a damper on lump-sum alimony settlements.

The third general requirement is that the alimony settlement must be a written instrument that is legally enforceable. This "in writing" requirement is imposed by subsection 71(b)(1)(A) and is defined by subsection 71(b)(2)(A). These subsections read —

(1)(A) Such payment is received by (or on behalf of) a [former] *spouse under a divorce or separation instrument.*
*(2)A) The term "divorce or separation instrument" means a decree of divorce or separate maintenance or a **written instrument** incident to such a decree.* [Emphasis added.]

The tax reason for the written instrument is so that the parties (and their attorneys) cannot change the alimony terms at will. Changes can be made, but only upon judicial modifications to the decree . . . after a court hearing.

An enforceable written instrument is helpful to the payee in the event of alimony arrears. Legal action can be taken to enforce collection of the arrears. If the arrears become substantial, and the payee takes no legal action, the IRS can *impute payment received* and assess the payee with tax. The IRS rationale for imputing (asserting) alimony arrears received is that there could be some substitute arrangement between the parties which is not in writing.

Time Duration of Payments

In rare cases, alimony payments can go on for an indefinite period of time. The indefiniteness is terminated by death of the payee (but not death of the payer) or by remarriage of the payee (but not remarriage of the payer). Where a payee is physically or mentally disabled, and never remarries, alimony can become an ongoing legal obligation without end. Much depends on the length of the marriage, ages of the spouses, and their occupational skills (current or potential). The judicial objective is to try to limit the payment obligation to a reasonable period of time post-separation.

What is a reasonable period of time for a divorcing spouse to rehabilitate, retrain, and reacclimate himself/herself to the occupational rigors of everyday business? There is no answer in federal tax law. State law, employable skills, and the local economy provide the only clues. In general terms, a "reasonable period" is considered to be approximately 3 to 6 years after separation of the spouses. The period can be shorter or it can be longer. Whatever it is, it must be prescribed in the written instrument incident to the divorce.

Section 71(b)(1) of the tax code defines alimony or separate maintenance payments as—

(A) Such payment [as} is received by (or on behalf of) a spouse under a divorce or separation instrument,
(B) the . . . instrument does not designate such payment as a payment which is not includible in the gross income [of the payee] *. . . and not allowable as a deduction* [to the payer],
(C) . . . the payee spouse and the payer spouse are not members of the same household at the time such payment is made, and
(D) there is no liability to make any such payment for any period after the death of the payee spouse.

Thus, no time period whatsoever is specified. The only statutory cutoff time is death of the payee spouse. Otherwise, if the alimony (or separate maintenance) payments are *received* by the payee spouse, they are includible in that spouse's gross income (Section 71(a)) and deductible from the payer spouse's income (Section 215(a)). Accordingly, the "written instrument" designating the amount of alimony payments should be prepared with the above provisions in mind.

Must Exclude Child Support

When preparing an alimony settlement, great care should be exercised to avoid combining child support payments with alimony payments. There is a simple tax reason for this. Alimony payments are includible (meaning taxable) in the gross income of the payee. Child support payments, on the other hand, are *not* tax includible by the payee. They are tax free. This is so stated in Section 71(c): *Payments to Support Children—*

> *Subsection (a)* [inclusion of alimony in gross income] *shall **not** apply to that part of any payment which the terms of the divorce or separation instrument fix (in terms of an amount of money or a part of the payment) as a sum which is payable for the support of children of the payer spouse.* [Emphasis added.]

This section seems clear enough: child support payments are not tax includible. But note carefully the three-letter emphasized word: "fix." What does this word mean?

Subsection 71(c)(2) attempts to define "fix" as—

> *Any amount specified . . .* [that] *will be reduced on the happening of a contingency relating to a child (such as attaining a specified age, marrying, dying, leaving school, or a similar contingency), or at a time which can clearly be associated with a contingency.*

The tax problem with Section 71(c) is that state laws (properly so) encourage the continuing of family units following divorce. A family unit is a parent with one or more minor child in custody. This leads to the concept of "family support" whereby spousal support and child support are combined into one payment. Since the payment is combined alimony and child support, the payer takes a tax deduction for the total amount. However, the payee treats the total amount as tax free, and does not report it in gross income. This violates the computer-matching cross check of Figure 7.1. A "red flag" goes up. A proposed tax increase (and interrogation) is then sent to the payee spouse by the IRS.

To avoid this mixup in tax treatments between payer and payee, IRS Regulation 1.71-1(e) comes down hard on the payee. In pertinent part (slightly edited), Regulation 1.71-1(e): *Payments for support of minor children*, reads as follows:

> *Section 71(a) does not apply to that part of any periodic payment which . . . is specifically designated as a sum payable for the support of minor children of the payer. If, however, the periodic payments are received by the payee for the support and maintenance of the payee and of minor children of the payer without such specific designation of the portion for the support of such children, then the whole of such amounts is includible in the income of the payee as provided in section 71(a).* [Emphasis added.]

In other words, if the amount of child support is not fixed and specifically designated as such, the full amount of any payment of family support will be treated as alimony to the payee. That is, it is taxable to the recipient. The rationale for this treatment is that the recipient is free to spend the money as he/she sees fit. There are no fixed conditions for use of the money. The payee, therefore, pays tax unnecessarily on child support amounts.

"When in Doubt" Examples

Keep in mind at all times that this is a tax book. While we recognize and support the need for family identity following divorce, we do not encourage paying taxes on amounts which are not required to be taxed.

From the IRS's point of view, unnecessary taxation does not exist. Their position is that if a divorce payment is not *clear and specific*, it will be interpreted in a manner that will maximize total revenue from both the payer and payee.

To present an oversimplified example, consider a $500 per month family payment. It is unclear whether the amount is for alimony, or for child support, or a combination of both. When in doubt, the IRS holds that the $500 is child support by the payer. Hence, it is *not* deductible by the payer. The IRS then turns its hat around and holds that the $500 is alimony to the payee, which is fully taxable. This way, the IRS gets more tax from the payer than it should. And it also gets more tax from the payee than it should.

Suppose the divorce decree specifies that the $500 above is $200 alimony and $300 child support. This is clear and specific. The $200 alimony is deductible by the payer and includible by the payee. The $300 child support is not deductible by the payer, and is not includible by the payee. See how straightforward this is?

Suppose the payer pays a total of $350 per month under the terms above instead of $500. How much is alimony? How much is child support?

Answer: $50 is alimony; $300 is child support. There is $150 per month alimony arrearage.

When in doubt, child support gets priority. This is so directed (but not very clearly) by Section 71(c)(3), to wit:

If any payment is less than the amount specified in the instrument, then so much of such payment as does not exceed the sum payable for support [of children of the payer] *shall be considered as payment for* [child] *support.*

Suppose now the payer pays a total of $650 per month instead of $500. How much is alimony? How much is other?

Answer: $200 is alimony; $300 is child support; and $150 . . . who knows?

The $150 could be a gift to the former spouse; it could be a gift to the child (or children). The $150 also could be a property settlement payment or payment on some ongoing debt obligation of the payer which has been advanced by the payee. Or, the $150 could be a makeup for some alimony arrearage of the past. If left up to the IRS, the $150 would be treated as a gift by the payer (not deductible) and as alimony to the payee (tax includible).

Do you see now why we stressed the importance of separate documentation in the tax arenas of divorce (back in Chapter 2: Figure 2.5)? Unless spouses and their attorneys are tax alert, the IRS will always win on divorce issues. Divorce returns comprise "hot targets" for audit. In the process, the IRS pits one spouse against the other, thereby catching each off-guard.

Must Exclude Property Settlement

There is another win-win situation for the IRS: when property settlement payments are mixed in with alimony payments. Unlike alimony, property settlement can be prescribed in cash payments, property transfers, notes of indebtedness, and substitutions of all sorts. All we want you to know at this time is that property settlement can include cash payments made simultaneously with alimony payments.

The purpose of alimony payments is to settle marital rights. The purpose of property transfers is to settle property rights. The two settlements involve entirely different tax arenas and rules. If structured correctly, property settlement can be a totally tax-free exchange of property interests between divorced spouses. Such is not the case with alimony.

Because of the potential tax-free aspects of property settlement, there is temptation to mix property transactions with alimony payments. If this can be done tax-unobtrusively, the payer spouse has the most to gain. He (she) would get a tax deduction for the whole affair. Consequently, the payer spouse and his/her attorney are the most likely to scramble property and alimony settlements in an underhanded — perhaps even fraudulent — way.

The scrambling/mixing of property payments with alimony is done by the technique of "front-loading." That is, the combined payments are loaded in the early post-divorce years, and taper off in the later years. Front-loading is presumed to exist when the payments decrease by more than $15,000 in a subsequent calendar year. The excess amount over $15,000 is *deemed to be* property settlement payments rather than alimony payments.

To illustrate the amount of excess front-loading, consider payments in year 1 to be $60,000; year 2 to be $35,000; and year 3 to be $10,000. The excess front-loading in year 1 is $60,000 less the *sum* of $35,000 (year 2) plus $15,000. Thus, the year 1 excess amount is $10,000 ($60,000 less $50,000). The excess in year 2 is also $10,000 ($35,000 less $10,000 less $15,000). And so on.

The rules on front-loading of alimony are very complex. They are set forth in Section 71(f), subsections (2) through (6): *Recomputation where Excess Front-Loading of Alimony*

Payments. The recomputation (recapture) status is the 3rd post-separation year . . . and is retroactive to the 1st and 2nd post-separation years. We will not discuss these rules any further, because it is so easy to avoid them. Simply do not propose or accept any alimony schedule where the payments increase or decrease by more than $15,000 from one year to the next.

Lump-Sum Settlements

Generally, alimony payments stop automatically upon remarriage of the payee spouse. But what happens if the payee is non-remarriageable or non-employable?

Answer: The alimony payments go on forever! "Forever" means until death of the payee.

In some divorce situations, the payee spouse is truly non-remarriageable and/or non-employable. There could be religious reasons, physical disabilities, nervous breakdown, mental disorder, absence of employable skills, or deep emotional bitterness, any of which might flash danger signals to prospective new spouses and to prospective employers. For these and other reasons, the payer spouse may much prefer a lump-sum alimony settlement. He/she wants to get rid of the alimony burden once and for all.

In these cases, usually, there is no ambiguity or scrambling with property settlement matters. The marital settlement offer is pure alimony. It is simply expressed as a fixed principal amount (for example: $200,000) payable in one or more installments. It is not broken down into dollars per month.

What is the tax treatment in this case?

If the lump sum were paid in one cash installment, the excess over $15,000 would **not** be treated as alimony. In other words, if the settlement were for $200,000, the amount of $185,000 would not be deductible to the payer, nor would it be includible by the payee. This treatment results from the application of Section 71(f) for the prevention of front-loading.

Obviously, a payer spouse is not going to willingly forego a $185,000 alimony deduction. To retain his deduction, he would seek to program his lump-sum settlement into approximately equal annual installments (say $20,000 per year . . . or whatever). But since he does not want to be reminded annually of his alimony obligation, what payment arrangements can he make?

In most lump-sum settlements, the payer arranges for cash installments to be paid from an annuity contract, life endowment, or alimony trust. Collectively, these are "trust entities." Arrangements are made with a financial institution for a corporate trustee to dispense the installments as contracted. The payments are made directly to the payee spouse.

The lump-sum amount is transferred by the payer to the trust entity. Although some initial cash is transferred, the predominant portion in the agreed amount is in the form of property, securities, debt instruments, and other funding vehicles. These transfers become trust assets known as corpus or principal. While being held for long-term payout, these trust assets generate income of their own. This income is taxable to whom?

The income — not the principal — is taxable to the beneficiary of the trust entity. This is the payee spouse, provided payment derives from a pure alimony trust. If any principal is included in the cash payments, the principal portion is not taxed to the payee.

This point is made quite clear in Section 682(a): *Income of an Estate or Trust in Case of Divorce, Etc.* In pertinent part, this section reads—

> *There shall be included in the gross income of a* [payee] *who is divorced or legally separated under a decree of separate maintenance . . . the amount of the income of any trust which such* [payee] *is entitled to receive and which, except for this section, would be includible in the gross income of the* [payer].

What about the payer spouse?

Those assets (corpus principal) transferred to the trust entity are not — repeat, *not* — tax deductible by the payer! The reason for this is that the cash payments are made by an entity: not by an individual. Section 215(a) clearly says: "In the case of an *individual*, there shall be allowed as a deduction . . . ."

Section 215(a) was intentionally enacted to put a damper on lump-sum settlements. These settlements tend to be more like property settlements, rather than alimony. The idea behind allowing a deduction for alimony is to make it (more or less) an *income equalizer* between divorcing spouses. Consequently, alimony payments are deductible only if they are made from sources of income ordinarily taxable to the payer.

This point is also reiterated in Section 215(d): *Coordination with Section 682.* That is—

No deduction shall be allowed under [Section 215(a)] *with respect to any payment if, by reason of Section 682 (relating to income of alimony trusts), the amount thereof is not* [construed as being] *includible in such individual's* [the payer's] *gross income* [before the trust is created].

In other words, the payer spouse gets no deduction for alimony payments made from sources of income which are not ordinarily taxable to him. This brings us back to the basic principle and message of this chapter. Qualified alimony payments are deductible from the gross income of the payer, and are includible in the gross income of the payee. No other payment arrangements count. See Figure 7.2 in this regard. Particularly note that child support and property settlement arrangements are outside of the realm of payments classed as "alimony." Our Figure 7.2 depiction is what properly should take place.

A Brazen Example

Some payers, when burdened with a large spousal settlement (alimony and property) seek to structure the obligation as income to the payee which is fully deductible by the payer. The persons who do so are generally highly-paid professionals: attorneys, doctors, CEOs , etc. These persons often are brazen and fearless. They ignore federal tax law: they use state contract law to subvert the tax rules. Here's a true case on point (of which the author has first-hand knowledge).

The payer, a multi-millionaire attorney, prepared all of the underlying legal papers relative to his divorce. Since no minor children were involved, he couched the alimony and property settlement terms in ambiguous and circuitous wording. After

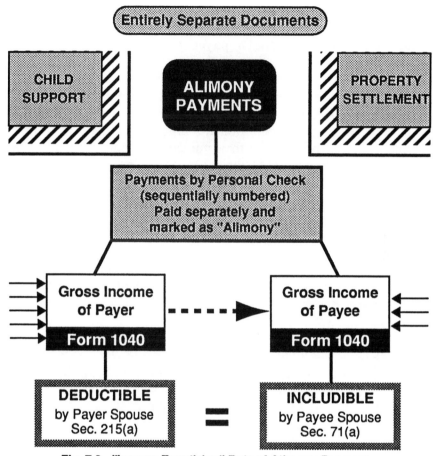

Fig. 7.2 - "Income Equalizing" Role of Alimony Payments

several years of legal wrangling, the lump-sum amount came to $2,750,000.

The attorney payer borrowed the $2,750,000 from a bank, using his $35,000,000 of real estate holdings as security. He invested the $2,750,000 to support himself; he did not pay off his ex-spouse. In the legal papers that followed, he subordinated his ex-spouse's obligation of $2,750,000 to the bank's obligation of the same amount. He did this by assigning the two debt obligations to a so-called: Irrevocable Family Trust. His entire $35,000,000 of real estate holdings was also transferred into the trust. No federal transfer tax was paid, whatsoever. His six adult children were the true beneficiaries of the trust.

His ex-spouse became a payee of the trust. This was accomplished by treating her as a *nonemployee*. Ordinarily, a nonemployee is an independent contractor who performs personal services for a payer. As such (normally), the payee pays income tax on "compensation"; the payer gets a business income tax deduction.

The payee dutifully reported the amount received as "other income": **not** alimony. She then immediately backed it out as a *mischaracterized payment* by the payer. It was property settlement and, therefore, not taxable to her. The IRS audited the payee for each of **three** separate years . . . and agreed! In the early negotiating legal papers, she had (via her attorney) waived all alimony payments and agreed only to the $2,750,000 property settlement.

For 12 years (as of this writing), the payer has gotten away with treating the payee payments as tax deductible to him. The IRS can't — or won't — touch him!

Why?

Because by being his own legal strategist, he keeps the payee payments issue tied up in state courts. It is IRS policy that when the characterization of a payment is pending in state court, the IRS waits until the state law issue is settled. In the situation above, the payments issue will not be settled until the payee spouse dies (about 20 years hence).

8

PROPERTY DISCLOSURE

Each Divorcing Spouse Is Required To Disclose All Of His/Her/Their Property Interests During The Marriage. This Involves Detailed Property Listings With Itemized Valuations. Each Spouse Independently Should Prepare A Listing Of Marital Property. Traceable Separate Property Of Either Spouse Is Excluded. After Consolidation Of Input From Both Spouses, The "Financial Net Worth" Of The Marital Estate Is Established. Before Any Final Division Of The Property, A "Cash Pool" — For EQUALIZING PURPOSES — Needs To Be Created. Otherwise, A "Hostage Asset" Has To Be Held To The Bitter End.

Before a marriage can be dissolved legally, there must be full disclosure of all property under the dominion and control of the divorcing spouses. The disclosure is necessary in order to arrive at an equitable distribution of that property, to satisfy the debts of the marriage, and to rearrange legal ownership and responsibility subsequent to the divorce.

For example, certain property may be 50/50 jointly owned during the marriage. After the divorce, one spouse may own it entirely, or both may own it fractionally (non-50/50), or the property may be sold and the net proceeds split 50/50 or non-50/50, as appropriate. Ownership of property sets the liability clock in motion under state law, and sets the tax clock in motion under federal law. The tax consequences on the split-up of marital property will differ substantially between spouses after divorce.

The term "property" means all assets and all liabilities of the divorcing spouses, of any kind, wherever situated. "Any kind" means real, personal, tangible, and intangible property items. "Wherever situated" means anywhere in the world, belonging to one spouse and/or the other.

The term "disclosure" means a complete inventory of all property items of value (those which could be sold on the retail market for $100 or more). Certain items of property have no market value to third-party interests, and therefore need not be disclosed. These include such close personal items as ordinary clothing, utensils, linens, photographs, handicrafts, and other memorabilia of the marital family. Everything else of value must be disclosed.

Key Reference Dates

When petition for divorce has been filed in the proper court, both petitioner and respondent have the right (under state law) to seek and insist on full disclosure of all property interests by the other. This is an inherent right under property laws of each state. The same rights would apply to two persons who were not husband and wife, where property issues are at stake. It is important to recognize that this right of disclosure is independent of the issues of marital rights and conflicts.

To unclog the emotional blockages between divorcing spouses, it is helpful to think only in terms of key reference dates. After all, disclosure does not mean all property ever owned at any time in one's life, from date of birth on. The disclosure is limited to those property interests referenced to certain specific dates.

What are the key reference dates?

Essentially, there are three such dates, namely:

One. *Date of marriage.* This commences the marital community and the process of commingling "his" and "hers" into a joint estate.

Two. *Date of separation.* This fixes a point in time when the marital estate ceases, and removes the issue of commingling from property disclosures.

Three. *Separate property date(s).* This is the date or dates on which separate property was acquired outside of the marital estate. There can be much difficulty in convincingly establishing such date or dates.

The date of marriage is the easiest to reference. It is clearly displayed on a couple's marriage license or certificate. It is an officially recorded date. From this date forward, all property items acquired from the combined incomes of husband and wife are *marital property*, pure and simple. This is so for federal tax purposes, regardless of whether married and/or domiciled in a community property or noncommunity property state. This is particularly so where a joint federal return was filed for the year of marriage and for all subsequent marital years.

The date of separation has to be a legal date. While the spouses may separate voluntarily, such date has no legal effect for property disclosure purposes. The date must be recognized judicially in the court where petition for divorce is filed. The court-recognized date of separation terminates property interest in the marital estate only. It has no bearing, per se, on the legal status of marriage. The parties involved cannot remarry at this point. The date of separation is merely a property accounting date. It forms the basis on which the subsequent disposition of marital property is made. It is that date which appears on a petition for divorce.

Separate Property Interests

The date or dates of separate property interests are "legal" only if the acquisition(s) are documented by third-party witnesses. For example, a husband buys 100 shares of stock from proceeds from a trust his parents (or other relatives) set up. The distribution from the trust is a documentable third-party date, as well as the purchase of the 100 shares (through a licensed broker). However, if the 100 shares were issued in the joint names of the husband and wife, instead of the husband only, the separate property date will have terminated. The property would be treated as *commingled property*, indistinguishable from marital property. Therefore, great care is required to keep separate that property which is truly separate.

Altogether, there are six possible classes of separate property dates. These are—

1. property acquired by gift,
2. property acquired by inheritance,
3. property acquired from trust (set up outside of marriage)
4. property acquired before marriage,
5. property acquired with separate funds while married, and
6. property acquired after the date of separation but before the final divorce decree (unless otherwise spelled out in a legal separation or separate maintenance order).

All such dates must be fully traceable via third-party documents, from date of acquisition to date of disclosure. The longer a marriage, the more difficult it is to establish such dates.

Figure 8.1 is presented as an aid to comprehending the importance of the above reference dates. Note that the separate property dates are arranged into Categories I and II. Category I is property acquired from sources other than the incomes of the spouses involved. Category II is that property acquired from spousal incomes under separate circumstances. If these dates can be convincingly traced, the underlying assets become *exclusionary property*. That is, such property is excluded from the marital property accounting.

Tracing Separate Property

In most states, there is an overriding legal presumption concerning the property holdings of husband and wife. From date of marriage to date of (legal) separation, all property interests are *presumed* to be marital property. As such, it is subject to equitable distribution upon divorce. This presumption prevails unless separate property claims can be clearly — and convincingly — traced. In most marital situations, tracing separate property is no easy task.

Let us illustrate the tracing problems with shares of stock. It could be any form of property interest: land, bank account, auto, business, residence, and so on. The tracing problem is the same.

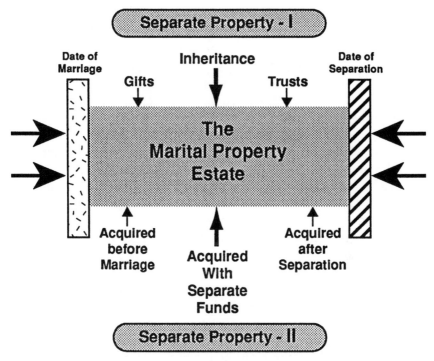

Fig. 8.1 - Reference Dates for Disclosing Property Interests

Consider an unmarried man who purchased 100 shares of ABC mutual fund at $10 per share. He paid $1,000 (100 sh x $10/sh) from his earnings. A year or so later, the ABC shares increased in value to $15 per share. He bought another 100 shares with $1,500 which he withdrew from his savings. He then had 200 ABC shares of separate property. Shortly thereafter, he got married.

The ABC shares continued to increase in value. This time, he and his wife together bought 200 more shares at $20 per share. They paid the $4,000 from their joint earnings. Two years later, the husband inherited $10,000 from his mother. By now, the ABC shares had increased to $25. The husband bought another 200 shares (cost $5,000) in joint tenancy with his wife, and put the balance of his inheritance ($5,000) in a joint savings account with his wife. A few years later, the shares had increased in value to $40. By this time there were 600 shares for a total value of $24,000.

Without warning, the wife filed a petition for divorce and moved out of the house. Her attorney sent a written demand to the husband for $12,000 cash for her "half" of the ABC stock.

How does the husband trace his separate property in this case?

The 200 shares bought before his marriage are clearly separate property. BUT does he have any canceled checks, savings withdrawal slips, or confirmation receipts showing when he bought the shares and how much he paid? Chances are, he misplaced (lost) the receipts when he moved from his bachelor's apartment into the marital residence. When he got married, he changed the account name to husband and wife. The presumption, therefore, is that the 200 shares is marital property. He tacitly gifted to his wife 100 of the 200 shares.

The 200 shares purchased as husband and wife are clearly marital property. No problem here: 100 shares are "his" and 100 shares are "hers."

The 200 shares which he bought with his inheritance are separate property. BUT, the fact that he put the shares in joint tenancy with his wife was clearly an intentional gift to her of 100 shares. There are no tax restrictions on interspousal gifting.

Actually, 400 shares were separate property, 200 were joint property (total 600). Had he kept proper documentation on the purchase of his separate shares, and had he kept them in his separate name, he then would have to fork over only $4,000 (100 sh x $40/sh) to his wife — instead of $12,000.

Agreement on Separate Property

Suppose the husband and wife above were amicable and civil towards each other. Neither is trying to take advantage of the other. If so, they could work out an agreement between themselves as to what constitutes the separate property of each.

In the illustration above, the wife knows in her heart that the 200 shares purchased before marriage are her husband's separate property. The fact that he changed the account to both names after marriage was an act of good faith and trust. It was not a tacit gift, as is legally presumed. A reasonable spouse could agree to this in writing, in good faith.

The wife above also knows that the 200 shares bought with the $5,000 of the husband's $10,000 inheritance is his separate property. He put the shares in joint tenancy as a matter of convenience only. Had he died before divorce, he certainly would want her to benefit from those shares without the necessity of probate. Again, a reasonable spouse could agree in writing, as a matter of convenience.

The $5,000 of the husband's inheritance that went into joint savings is another matter. It is not separate property. Portions of the money were used for household furnishings, for vacations, and for theater/sports events. The obvious intent was to derive mutual benefit through marital consumption. The husband, being a reasonable person, would make no claim on this $5,000. Whatever is left in the joint savings account at time of separation would be the marital property of both spouses.

For the situation above, an agreement on separate property could be a simple statement along the lines presented in Figure 8.2. A similar agreement could also be written in language identifying any separate property of the wife.

Where each spouse has his/her separate property which can be mutually agreed upon, it is best to have *two* Figure 8.2-type documents: one for the husband ("his") and one for the wife ("hers"). Each agreement should be signed by each spouse in the presence of a Notary Public. This can avoid confusion later on.

There is one precaution about entering into an agreement as to separate property. It should be limited strictly to clearly identifiable separate property items. **It should not be an agreement to distribute any of the marital property.** Such a distribution will come later, after full disclosure of all marital property items. Any separate property would be excluded from the marital property disclosures and divisions.

Overview of Marital Property Items

If the tracing of separate property cannot be convincingly documented, or if no agreement on separate property can be reached, it is then better to concede that all items are marital property. The longer the marriage, the easier and more convenient it

---

SEPARATE PROPERTY AGREEMENT

We, ___(husband)___ and ___(wife)___ , hereby agree that the following items are the separate property of ___(husband)___ , namely:

(1) 200 shares of ABC purchased by ___(husband)___ , prior to the date of our marriage.

(2) 200 shares of ABC purchased by ___(husband)___ with funds inherited from his late mother during our marriage.

We acknowledge that a petition for dissolution of our marriage has been filed, and that we separated from each other on ___(date)___ .

This agreement is executed under our mutual free will, without duress, menace, fraud, or undue influence of one upon the other.

Executed this _____ day of ___(month)___ , ___(year)___ at ___(city)___ , ___(state)___ .

Notary Public

_____ /s/
(husband)

_____ /s/
(wife)

Fig. 8.2 - Example of Voluntary Separate Property Agreement

is to justify so conceding. If one spouse does not voluntarily concede, attorney fees and court litigation can go on and on. (Recall our "brazen example" in the latter part of Chapter 7.) In the end, the presumption of marital property interests from date of marriage to date of separation will most likely prevail.

Before marital property can be equitably distributed, it must be fully and adequately disclosed. The disclosure process is initiated by a declaratory listing of all such property: "his," "hers," and "theirs." The term "all" means everything of value, of any kind, anywhere located where an ownership interest of one or both spouses is at stake. This includes personal property (furniture, furnishings, jewelry), tangible property (vehicles, equipment), intangible property (cash, savings, securities, insurance), real property (buildings and structures attached to land), business property (inventory, accounts receivable, machinery, fixtures), and all marital debts (mortgages, charge accounts, loans). How short or long the declaratory listing is will depend on the wealth and duration of each marital estate.

When the spouses separate with the intention of remaining separate, each is expected to itemize what he *and* she believes is the marital estate. In other words, two separate itemized listings: one prepared by the husband, and one prepared by the wife. In this manner, there is a cross check on the two spousal listings. Human nature is such that any two persons are going to have different points of view. So cross-checking is an essential ingredient to the adequate disclosure of all marital property.

As a guide towards what is required in the value listing of marital property items, Figure 8.3 is presented. The information in Figure 8.3 is not exhaustive. But it does cover the main classes of property, so that each spouse can amplify as is appropriate to his or her own marital case. Chances are, many marital property items would never be sold. Nevertheless, they must be valued as though they were to be sold.

How Value Ascertained

"Value" is something that can be ascertained in a retail market. It represents the amount of money that a buyer would be willing to pay for each item offered, having reasonable knowledge of its condition and location. In the tax and business world, this concept is referred to as *fair market value*. The word "fair" presumes that there is a competition among buyers which eliminates bargains, forced sales, manipulations of terms, or purchase made under compulsion or unusual circumstances.

Value has to be ascertainable in a specific number of dollars for each separate item capable of being offered for sale. It does not matter whether an item of property is actually being offered. The fact that some ordinary buyer would be willing to pay for it means that value can be ascertained. As a practical matter, however, if an item is less than $100 in value, it can be ignored for purposes here.

The process of valuation of property in estate matters is set forth in IRS Regulation 20.2031-1(b). This is a very lengthy tax regulation, but the points pertinent to our discussion here are as follows:

	ITEM OF PROPERTY	DESCRIPTION & LOCATION	MKT VAL.	SUPPORTING DOCUMENTS
1	VEHICLES	Auto, boat, trailer, camper, airplane, motorcycle, etc.	$ Each Item	Dealer "blue book", newspaper ads, etc.
2	EQUIPMENT	Hunting, fishing, machinery, tractors, tools, computers, cellular phones, etc.	$ Each Item	Purchase receipts, sales catalogs, etc.
3	SPECIAL ITEMS	Collectibles, (watches, guns, stamps) art objects, TV, stereo, VCR, DVD, etc.	$ Each Item	Professional app-raisals, statements by dealers, etc.
4	ANIMALS	Horses, exotic housepets, breeders, cages, harnesses, etc.	$ Each Item	Estimates from pet stores, clinics, reg-istration services
5	HOUSEHOLD ITEMS	Furniture, furnishings, kitchen-ware, appliances (large and small), fixtures, etc.	$ Each Item	Newspaper class-ified ads, used furn-iture shops
6	INSURANCE	Life insurance, employer pensions, deferred annuities, profit sharing plans	$ Each Item	Cash value of in-surance, vested interest in pensions
7	CASH & SECURITIES	Savings, checking, money markets, stock, bonds, mutual funds, trust deeds, etc.	$ Each Item	Photocopies of acc-ount balances, finan-cial sec.of paper, etc.
8	REAL ESTATE	Residence, land, rentals, commercial property, historic structures, etc.	$ Each Item	Professional app-raisals, recent comp-arable sales, etc.
9	BUSINESS INTERESTS	Proprietorships (trade, business, professional), part-nerships, joint ventures	$ Each Item	Book values plus prof. and other app-raisals & statements
10	DEBTS	Mortgages, loans payable, notes payable, judgments, credit cards, charge accts., etc.	$ Each Item	Photocopies of acct. balances, spec-ific inquiries to creditors, etc.

Fig. 8.3 - Disclosure by Value Listing All Marital Property

The value of every item of property includible in a [marital] *gross estate . . . is its fair market value at the time of the* [separation of spouses]. *The fair market value of a particular item of property . . . is not to be determined by a forced sales price. Nor is* [it] *to be determined by the sale of the item in a market other than that in which such item is most commonly sold to the public, taking into account the location of the item wherever appropriate. All relevant facts and elements of values of the applicable valuation date . . . [such as] description, make, model, age, condition, etc. . . . . shall be considered in every case.*

In essence, Regulation 20.2031-1(b) means that for a marital disclosure listing such as Figure 8.3, a conscientious effort must be made to assign an ascertainable value to each item of property. For most of the items, one is concerned with valuing used property. Such values can be quite readily established by comparison with like property in the classified section of local newspapers or downloaded from relevant Internet listings. It is helpful to collect these printed sources for a period of 60 day prior to date of separation, through 60 days after date of separation. Then circle in red (or other prominent color) each comparable property item, and the date and price it is offered for sale. This valuation procedure is not beyond challenge, but it does establish conscientious intent.

Where there is an active used property market (such as autos, campers, equipment, etc.), local dealers can be visited for on-the-spot value comparisons. Where appropriate, written estimates and/or printed flyers can be obtained. These local visits may include secondhand stores, specialty shops, Salvation Army outlets, flea markets, junk dealers, and the like. Not to be overlooked are personal bulletin board for-sale ads posted at local food markets, shopping centers . . . and on the Internet.

In the case of stocks, bonds, securities, trust deed notes, life insurance, pensions, annuities, and the like, brokers and agents in these fields should be contacted. Written estimates can be obtained, in some cases without payment or fees. Where employer benefit plans are involved, the employer should be contacted for a statement of one's nonforfeitable vested interest in such plan(s).

In the case of real estate, antiques, and collectibles (coins, guns, jewelry, etc.), the services of professional appraisers are required. Such appraisals can be obtained for reasonable fees. Appraisers will provide written substantiation of their estimates, and will stand behind the figures . . . in court if necessary. Most such appraisers have practical experience in public auctions. For other comparable appraisals, visiting a public auction house can be helpful.

Where accounts are maintained at banks, savings institutions, mutual funds, brokerage firms, and the like, photocopies of the account balances are required as of date of separation. The same photocopying requirement applies to all billings on marital debts (mortgages, loans, credit cards, charge accounts, etc.).

The whole idea above is for *each spouse* to prepare a value listing of all property within their marital estate. Each should do this, separately and independently of the other. In this manner, what one spouse overlooks, the other may not. Where one spouse may overestimate or underestimate, the other spouse becomes a counter check-and-balance. Ultimately, both spouses will split the total property interests equitably. Because so, there is no vindictiveness to be gained by biasing the values, in favor of or against, one spouse or the other.

Consolidation Procedures

Once each spouse has prepared his/her separate Figure 8.3-type value listing, the next step is to consolidate the two lists into one. That is, ultimately one list will be used as the common basis for an equitable settlement of the property interests between the spouses. The hope is that both spouses can agree to the contents of the one listing and to the reasonableness of the values itemized.

To consolidate two separate spousal property listings into one, the services of a third party professional are required. The third party should *not* be an attorney, regardless of whether "his" or "hers." Attorneys tend to haggle too much over fine points and picky issues. Nor should the third party be any kind of sales agent or broker who would derive a commission from the sale of any property items listed. This pretty well rules out insurance agents, stock brokers, real estate persons, financial planners, and the like.

Preferably, the third party should be an independent professional working on a consulting basis only. This would include tax preparers, accountants, property appraisers, business specialists, engineers, and the like. These persons are familiar with collecting and sorting numbers. They are familiar with detailed itemizations and cost estimating procedures. They know how to probe for hidden assets and undisclosed liabilities of the marriage. They are capable of give and take in consolidating different figures and different points of view. They have a natural sense for the end goal: a bottom line *net worth* value (assets minus liabilities) for the marital estate.

After the consolidator does all that he can to pull together all of the appropriate property items, he prepares a "first draft" of the consolidated list. A copy of the first draft is given to each spouse for examination and — hopefully — concurrence. Some spouses review the consolidated listing with their attorneys. This can be helpful to attorneys since most of the dog work is done. Either attorney can add to, change, or take from the list as proper.

If there is a dispute between the spouses and/or their attorneys concerning any item on the consolidated list, the matter can be resolved in court. There is no need to take up court time for each and every item on the list. Concentrate on the one or two property items and their values for which there are genuine, good faith differences. The courts tend to resolve such differences by middle-ground compromise.

Importance of "Cash Pool"

Marital property settlements are usually delayed for one practical reason. Money. That is, lack of money. Most marriages on the rocks are cash short. Consequently, a marriage cannot be finally dissolved until there is adequate cash available to equalize the property distributions between spouses.

In most cases, one or two high-value items constitute the lion's share of the marital net worth. Often, this is the marital residence. But it may also be other real estate (such as farm land or rental units), or other ownership interests (such as a proprietorship business or partnership). These and similar property interests cannot be split down the middle or divided into subparts.

The solution is a distribution plan whereby one spouse gets a relatively larger share of cash, and the other gets a relatively larger share of noncash. To accomplish this, a *cash pool* is necessary.

There are several ways to generate a cash pool. The most obvious is to refinance the marital residence: get a "home equity loan." The refinancing should be done while the spouses are legally husband and wife. Even though physically separated for tax and support reasons, they are still legally married. They can co-sign the refinance papers in good faith. Until the divorce is final, they are both co-liable to the mortgage lender.

Another way is to use readily marketable assets such as stocks, bonds, mutual fund shares, trust deed notes, etc. as collateral for a cash pool loan. Or, one can borrow against his/her life insurance or pension plan.

Another way to create a cash pool is to sell off some of the marital property items in the consolidated list. As selected items are sold, the list has to be revised. The net worth bottom line, however, should not be too greatly affected. If the estimated values of the listed property items are realistic, the process is merely the substitution of cash for noncash.

As the conversion to cash proceeds, the money should be put into an interest-bearing demand account (savings or money market) to be disbursed at time of final decree. The account should be set up under the jurisdiction of the divorce court, and should require two signatures for withdrawal. One signature would be that of a trustee for the husband; the other, that of a trustee for the wife.

9

PROPERTY SETTLEMENT

If Handled Separately From Child Support And Alimony Payments, Property Settlement Between Spouses Or Former Spouses Is Treated As A TAX-FREE Exchange. This Is The Consequence Of Section 1041: *Transfers Of Property Between Spouses Or Incident To Divorce.* The Term "Incident To" Can Mean Up To 6 Years After Cessation Of The Marriage. As Two Published Court Rulings Reveal, Strict Property Accounting And Titling Rules Apply. When Preparing The FINAL Decree, Attorneys Often Fail To Cite The Impact Of Section 1041, Especially For Settlements Which Involve Transfers Into A Trust.

Property settlement is the dividing up of the marital estate, and distribution of designated items to each of the divorcing spouses. Upon distribution, each has exclusive physical, legal, and economic control over his/her property items. No longer is there co-ownership . . . nor is there co-liability. The distributed property belongs to each spouse as though they had never married.

There may, or may not be, tax consequences at the final distribution. Much depends on the nature of the property, and on how the distribution is made. Ideally, if made as an equal-value distribution of the entire estate, it would be a pure tax-free transaction. For various practical reasons, an equal-value distribution is rarely ever made. This leaves many divorced spouses up in the air as to the tax status of their property exchanges.

The tax treatment of property settlement between husband and wife has been a grey area of long standing. It boils down to the question of ownership (and timing of the distributions). What are the ownership rights of each spouse in the marital property? Are they co-owners equally; are they co-owners non-equally; or are they owner and non-owner with marital rights?

If husband and wife own the marital property co-equally (such as joint tenancy, tenants by the entirety, community property), any approximately equal settlement between them is a *division of property*; not a sale or exchange. If properly timed with the dissolution of marriage, the division is nontaxable.

If property is acquired after marriage, but in the husband's name only (under state law), does the wife have any ownership rights by virtue of marriage? What about right of support, right of use, right of inheritance, etc.? Are these property rights or are they marital rights? In such cases, can property rights and marital rights be distinguished as independent legal obligations?

Agreement on property settlement terms is generally the last phase of negotiations on divorce matters. By this time, child dependency issues are out of the way, and alimony payments have been thrashed out. These final negotiations can be stormy or peaceful. Much depends on the intelligence and maturity of each of the spouses . . . and their attorneys.

The Ideal Exemplified

It is possible — yes, it is — to arrange property settlement terms to be truly equal . . . for both spouses. A depiction of this ideal is presented in Figure 9.1. As can be noted, "his" share of the marital estate exactly equals "her" share . . . and vice versa.

We began setting the stage for this ideal arrangement in Chapter 8: Property Disclosure. At this point, we urge you to go back and glance at Figure 8.3 (on page 8-10). Particularly note the shaded column headed "MKT VAL" for Market Value. We purposely left it blank. Now, we want to fill it in.

Purely as a hypothetical illustration, we have divided up the marital property items as shown in Figure 9.2. Note that we have filled in the market value column and have set up a "Distribution"

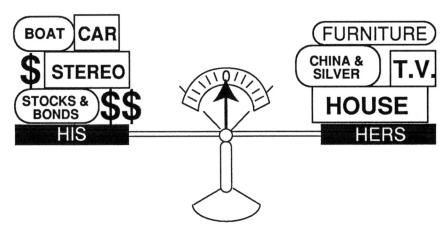

Fig. 9.1 - Ideal Property Distribution In Amicable Divorce

column as two subcolumns: Husband and Wife. The husband-wife division of property is such that each winds up getting exactly 50% of the marital net worth.

To be more specific, the net worth of the marital estate in Figure 9.2 is $136,480 (after mortgages and all other debts). Or, it could have been $1,136,480. Therefore, Figure 9.2 is illustrative only. Of the illustrated amount, the husband gets property, cash, and liabilities worth $68,240. The wife gets more property, less cash, and liabilities also worth $68,240. This is pure equality of division between spousal co-owners.

How did we achieve this pure equality of division?

It was not done on an item-by-item basis, nor by equality in kind. It was not done by going outside of the marital estate for borrowed money or promissory notes. It was all done within the marital estate. In our particular example, the marital residence was refinanced (see Item 5 in Figure 9.2) while the parties were legally husband wife (even though physically separated).

Look at the subtotals of the property item categories. None of the subtotals are equal between husband and wife. Yet — and this is the crucial point — the bottom line (net worth) totals of husband and wife are exactly equal.

We explained in Chapter 8 the importance of a cash pool generated *within* the marital estate. The cash pool is the property market-value "equalizer."

ITEM	Fair Market Value $	Distribution	
		Husband	Wife
1. **Vehicles**			
Auto 1	5,800	5,800	
- loan balance	(2,600)	(2,600)	
Auto 2	4,300		4,300
- loan balance	(1,600)		(1,600)
Subtotal	**5,900**	**3,200**	**2,700**
2. **Special Items**			
TV & Stereo	2,800	2,600	200
Jewelry	1,100	100	1,000
Fishing Gear	200	200	
Piano	600		600
Subtotal	**4,700**	**2,900**	**3,700**
3. **Household Items**			
Furniture	2,800	1,000	1,800
Furnishings	700	300	400
Kitchenware	800	300	500
Small appliances	900	700	200
Large appliances	1,400	600	800
Subtotal	**6,600**	**2,900**	**3,700**
4. **Cash & Securities**			
Checking Account	1,280	640	640
Savings Accunt	4,300	3,100	1,200
Company Pension	2,600		2,600
School Pension	7,500	7,500	
Refinance Cash	50,000	50,000	
Subtotal	**65,680**	**61,240**	**4,440**
5. **Residence**			
Appraised value	154,000		154,000
- 1st Mortgage	(42,600)		(42,600)
- 2nd Mortgage	(50,000)		(50,000)
Subtotal	**61,400**		**61,400**
6. **Debts**			
Credit Cards	(1,600)	(500)	(1,100)
Charge Accounts	(1,900)		(1,900)
Medical	(2,800)		(2,800)
Other	(1,500)	(1,500)	
Subtotal	**(7,800)**	**(2,000)**	**(5,800)**
TOTAL NET WORTH	**136,480**	**68,240**	**68,240**

Fig. 9.2 - Equal-Value Division of Total Marital Estate

In Figure 9.2, we gave the wife the residence. So, she wound up with more property in hand than the husband. We equalized this by giving the husband more cash than the wife. Compare Category 4 (Husband) with Category 5 (Wife). Note that this subdivision alone is approximately equal (less than 5% value difference). We could have done it the other way around: residence to the husband, cash to the wife. Much depends on which spouse has custody of any children.

The amount of actual cash (in Figure 9.2) to the husband is $50,000. Is there any tax on this $50,000?

No. It is tax free! This is true, believe it or not. No gimmicks.

The wife gets a $154,000 house with an offsetting $50,000 mortgage. So, instead of cash, she gets the cash equivalent in property: called "money's worth." Does she pay any tax on this additional $50,000 in money's worth?

No. She does not.

Both spouses come out of the Figure 9.2 deal tax free. Neither spouse is tax favored; neither spouse is tax injured. That is, neither is favored nor injured *at the time* of the property settlement. After the divorce, the tax situation will be much different, if and when any property items are sold.

In an amicable property settlement, the attorney preparing the final decree would recapitulate the division of property from a tabulation much like that of Figure 9.2. Chances are, he/she would prepare two separate tabulations: Exhibit A for husband and Exhibit B for wife. Exhibit A would be marked: "To Husband as his Separate Property"; and Exhibit B would be marked: "To Wife as her Separate Property." Each exhibit would be a detailed listing of each property item distributed and its fair market value. Wording on the property settlement agreement might go along the lines indicated in Figure 9.3.

Seldom Pure: Mostly Impure

The arrangements in Figures 9.1, 9.2, and 9.3 are *pure* property settlements. The purity is that all property acquired from date of marriage on, and in existence on date of separation, is co-owned

PROPERTY SETTLEMENT AGREEMENT

THIS AGREEMENT is made between _____ , as husband, and _____ , as wife. These parties were married on _____ , and separated on _____ .

DIVISION OF PROPERTY

Upon execution of this instrument, the marital property shall be distributed as follows:

    (a) Husband shall receive as his separate property all of those items set forth in Exhibit A attached hereto.

    (b) Wife shall receive as her separate property all of those items set forth in Exhibit B attached hereto.

PROPERTY WARRANTY

Each party warrants to the other that neither is possessed of any property of any kind that has not been fully disclosed to the other, and that has not been taken into account in the itemization of Exhibits A and B.

ENCUMBRANCES

The assignments of property in Exhibits A and B are subject to all existing encumbrances and liens thereon, including tax liens. The transferee agrees to indemnify and hold harmless the transferor from any claim or liability that may arise from said encumbrances and liens.

PROPERTY INSURANCE

All insurance is assigned to the party receiving the property in Exhibits A and B, and all premiums from the date hereof shall be paid by transferee.

DEBTS AND LIABILITIES

All debts, liabilities, and other obligations relative to the property in Exhibits A and B shall be borne by the transferee of that property, or as otherwise itemized on said exhibits. Each party hereby releases the other from any and all co-liability that might arise hereinafter from said debts and liabilities.

SEPARATE ACQUISITIONS

Any property acquired by either party after the date of separation set forth above, shall be the sole and separate property of the party acquiring it. The party not acquiring said property waives any and all rights to it by virtue of the marriage being now dissolved.

IN WITNESS WHEREOF this instrument is executed this _____ day of _____ , 20_____ .

Verification and Seal of Notary Public

/s/ _____
Husband

/s/ _____
Wife

Fig. 9.3 - Example Wording of an Amicable Property Settlement

equally between husband and wife. This is presumed so regardless of the state laws and regardless of in whose separate name (husband *or* wife) the property is actually titled. There is purity also in that matters of child support (if any) and alimony (if any) involve no property transfers of any kind.

There is further purity (in the ideal) in that the property settlement date is concurrent with the date of the final divorce decree. That is, following the legal date of dissolution of the marriage, there are no ongoing property transactions between the (former) spouses. The settlement is pure, equal, and tax-free (period)! Each separate owner takes on a "fresh start."

Pure property settlements in divorce are rare. We suspect that no more than 5% are pure in form. Over 90% are impure.

We use the term "impure" to imply a mixture of state law conflicts, marital and parental obligations, wrongdoing between attorneys, and ongoing property obligations between spouses after — sometimes long after — the final decree is issued.

Impurities arise for many reasons. The foremost reason is the antiquity of "separate property" state laws, and the inability of some state laws to distinguish between property rights of the husband and wife and the marital rights of husband and wife. For example, in some states spouse A may acquire property while married, in A's name only. Upon divorce, it becomes the separate property of A, but with certain marital rights attached. That is, during the marriage, spouse B acquires rights to use the property, to enjoy the income from it, to be gifted it, or to inherit it. These are more commonly called "beneficial rights" to property, rather than ownership rights. The trend is to treat marital rights to property as *a species of common ownership* — whereby each spouse is a part owner thereof. That is, during marriage, co-ownership of the commonly-used property is implied.

As a result, property settlements today more typically boil down to three distinct forms. These settlements are:

1. Equitable-value distributions
    — whereby all significant assets and liabilities are more or less equalized.
2. Negotiated settlements

       — whereby only major marketable assets are discussed and assigned.

  3. Commingled agreements

       — whereby the transferring spouse wants to "wrap" child support, alimony payments, and property exchanges into one package for the subsequent tax rearrangement of his choice. As implied in Figure 9.4, any commingling of the primary issues in divorce becomes a deliberate attempt to ambiguitize the tax treatment therewith.

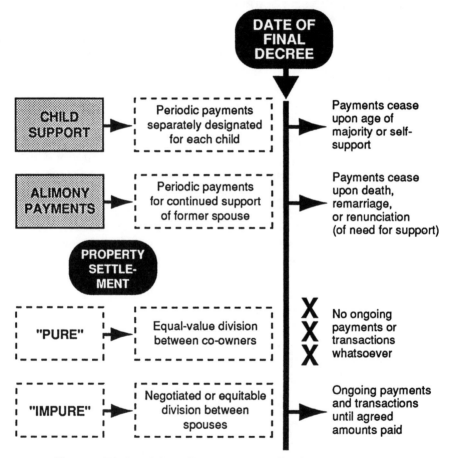

Fig. 9.4 - Distinguishing Features of the Key Issues in Divorce

Section 1041 Overview

The wrangling over the tax issues of property settlement matters has frustrated the IRS for many years. To put the issues to rest (hopefully), Section 1041 was enacted. This section is titled: *Transfers of Property Between Spouses or Incident to Divorce.* Section 1041 applies to all divorce property settlements taking place after July 18, 1984. This law has not been changed since.

As you may surmise on your own, the title of Section 1041 addresses two separate time spans. There is a time span of property exchanges "between spouses" and, separately, a time span "incident to divorce." The between-spouses time span is any time before the final decree of divorce and coincident with it. The span incident to divorce may extend up to six years after the marriage ceases.

The placement of Section 1041 in the Tax Code (and selected wording from it) is presented in Figure 9.5. Do note that Section 1041 appears in Part III of Subchapter O: *Common Nontaxable Exchanges.* Do not let the caption word "nontaxable" fool you. The term nontaxable does not mean tax-free forever. It means nontaxable only at the time the spouses are negotiating which items are "his" and which items are "hers." There is tax accountability somewhere down the line (after the divorce) when property is sold or exchanged to other than a former spouse.

The nontaxable character of property exchanges at time of divorce is confirmed in subsection 1041(a): **General Rule.** It reads in full:

No gain or loss shall be recognized on the transfer of property from an individual to (or in trust for the benefit of)—

> *(1) a spouse, or*

> *(2) a former spouse, but only if the transfer is incident to the divorce.* [Emphasis added.]

The term "gain or loss" refers only to property transactions where, but for Section 1041, capital gain or capital loss would be income tax recognized. Ordinarily, this would require the reporting

---

INTERNAL REVENUE CODE

Subtitle A - Income Taxes
Chapter 1 - Normal Taxes and Surtaxes

- -

Subchapter O - GAIN OR LOSS ON DISPOSITION OF PROPERTY
Part III - Common Nontaxable Exchanges

Section 1041 - Transfers of Property Between Spouses or Incident to Divorce

- -

Sub-section

(a) **General Rule.**

No gain or loss shall be recognized on a transfer of property from an individual to (or in trust for the benefit of) -
(1) a spouse, or (2) a former spouse, but only if the transfer is incident to the divorce.

(b) **Transfer Treated as Gift; Transferee has Transferor's Basis.**

In the case of any transfer of property described in subsection (a) -
(1) for purposes of this subtitle, the property shall be treated as acquired by the transferee by gift, and
(2) the basis of the transferee in the property shall be the adjusted basis of the transferor.

(c) **Incident to Divorce.**

For purposes of subsection (a) (2), a transfer of property is incident to the divorce if such transfer -
(1) occurs within 1 year after the date on which the marriage ceases, or
(2) is related to the cessation of the marriage.

(d) **Special Rule where Spouse is a Nonresident Alien.**

(e) **Transfers in Trust where Liability Exceeds Basis.**

Fig. 9.5 - Section 1041: Its Placement and Wording in Tax Code

of such transactions on Schedule D (Form 1040): Capital Gains and Losses. But under the incident-to-divorce provisions of Section 1041(a), no such Schedule D reporting is required. The rationale for not doing so derives from the principles of IRC Section 2523: Gift(s) to Spouse.

Treatment as Gift(s)

The tax characterization of transfers of property between divorcing spouses is that of interspousal *gifting* This is the significance of subsection 1041(b)(1): ***Transfer Treated as Gift.*** The precise statutory wording is—

> *In the case of any transfer of property described in subsection (a)—*
>> *(1) . . . the property **shall be treated** as acquired by the transferee* [recipient] *by **gift** . . .* [Emphasis added.]

In other words, between spouses, when any transfer of property is treated as a **gift,** it is not construed as a sale or exchange. Full and adequate consideration is deemed paid. Consequently, the transfer is not taxable . . . at the time of the gift. The nontaxing of interspousal gifts is a federal concept of long standing. The concept holds that a husband and wife are a single economic unit. As such, any transfers of property between them are simply different degrees of division among co-owners.

How does this gifting concept play out in real life, *before* divorce is final?

Answer: Amicable spouses — and, perhaps, not so amicable spouses who sense the tax benefits to each side — can work out their property settlement differences between themselves. They do not need attorneys to do what they can do on their own.

In a nutshell, subsections 1041(a)(1) and (b)(1) permit the spouses to do three things:

One. Section 1041 permits husband and wife to enter into *any kind of* written agreement to divide their marital property *any way* they want. They are not required to distinguish between marital rights and property rights. They can make any re-arrangements they want, so long as they identify every transaction in writing.

Two. The written agreement does *not* have to be prepared by an attorney. It can be prepared by themselves, by a nonattorney, or by a paralegal. The only requirement is that once the agreement is in writing, final divorce must ensue. If it does so, *for tax purposes*, it is immaterial whether the property settlement terms are incorporated in the final decree or not. It is highly advisable, of course, that the property settlement agreement be fully incorporated into the final decree.

Three. If all property transfers take place before the written agreement and within one year after it, there is no immediate income tax concern [subsec. 1041(c)(1)]. The transfers are nontaxable. They are nontaxable regardless of whether the property items were jointly owned or separately owned when gifted. Upon divorce (final decree), the parties are no longer spouses. Any property transfers thereafter are tax accountable; they may or may not be taxed, depending on the facts and circumstances then.

Meaning of "Incident to Divorce"

Subsection 1041(a)(**2**) above uses the phrase

a former spouse, but only if the transfer is incident to divorce.

In other words, the nontaxability of spousal exchanges may occur after the divorce is final . . . but only for certain time limits. Property settlement disputes cannot go on indefinitely. At some point, the tax ax must chop.

The after-divorce time limits are prescribed by subsection 1041(c): *Incident to Divorce*. This part of Section 1041 reads

For purposes of subsection (a)(2), a transfer of property is incident to the divorce if such transfer—

(1)   occurs within 1 year after the date on which the marriage ceases, or

(2)   is related to the cessation of marriage.

Paragraph 1041(c)(1) is self-explanatory. But what about paragraph (c)(2)? What is the meaning of "related to the cessation" in terms of a specific number of years of time?

To answer the "related to cessation" question, we must cite IRS Regulation § 1.1041-1T(b) Q-7: *When is a transfer of property "related to the cessation of the marriage"?*

The official answer is—

A transfer of property is treated as related to the cessation of the marriage if the transfer is pursuant to a divorce or separation instrument . . . and the transfer occurs ***not more than 6 years after*** *the date on which the marriage ceases.*

A 6 years "after" period is allowed for those cases where the transfers of property are hampered by ownership disputes, business impediments, disputes concerning the value of the property, and other extra-marital legal entanglements at the time of divorce. The presumption is that it could reasonably take up to 6 years after a divorce to work things out. The conclusion of the above cited regulation goes on to say—

Any transfer occurring more than 6 years after the cessation of the marriage is presumed to be not related to the cessation of the marriage.

Surely, six years after divorce is adequate time to work out all property settlement issues. When it is not, there is implication that the "deep pockets" spouse deliberately wants to torment his/her former spouse.

Transfers "For Benefit of" Spouse

Section 1041(a) directs attention to the transfer of property from an individual to . . . (*or in trust for the benefit of*) . . . a spouse (or former spouse). This clearly permits a transfer**or** spouse (the one giving up property) to assign it to a trust or other entity for the benefit of — or "on behalf of" — the transfer**ee** spouse (the recipient of the property). This raises the question: What are the trust-like arrangements that qualify for the no-gain-or-loss treatment under Section 1041?

Regulation § 1.1041-1T(c) Q/A-9 addresses this question specifically. This regulation points out that there are three situations in which transfers into a trust-like arrangement are qualifiable. These situations are:

1. Where the transfer to the third party (or entity) is *required* by a divorce decree or separation instrument.
2. Where the transfer to the third party is pursuant to the **written request** of the other spouse (or former spouse).
3. Where the transferor receives from the other spouse (or former spouse) a written **consent or ratification** of the transfer to the third party. Such consent or ratification **must state** that the parties intend the transfer to qualify under the rules of Section 1041.

The regulation goes on to say—

In the three situations described above, the transfer of property will be treated as **made directly to** *the nontransferring spouse (or former spouse) and the nontransferring spouse will be treated as immediately transferring the property to the third party. The deemed transfer* **from the** *nontransferring spouse (or former spouse) to the third party is* **not** *a transaction that qualifies for nonrecognition of gain under Section 1041.* [Emphasis added.]

To help you better understand this regulatory wording, we suggest you glance at our Figure 9.6. The arrangement is classed as a "deemed transfer." That is, even though the property is not transferred directly to the transferee spouse (the ultimate recipient), it is *deemed* to be so. Here the word "deemed" means "constructively received." That is, the transferee has beneficial access to the property more or less at will. Note in Figure 9.6 that the "1st leg" of the deemed transfer is nontaxable, whereas the "2nd leg" is taxable. Why do you suppose the 2nd leg is taxable?

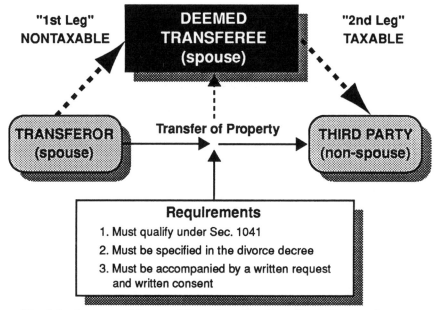

Fig. 9.6 - Concept of Deemed Transfers "for Benefit of" Former Spouse

Underlying the nontaxability of the 1st leg is the requirement that the transferred property qualifies precisely under Section 1041. The dollar amount(s) must be spelled out and the transfer obligation must be mandatory. Otherwise, any **excess property** transfer is taxable.

For example, suppose a property settlement agreement required the husband to transfer $250,000 of property or its equivalent into trust or other entity for the benefit of his wife (or former wife). Instead, suppose he transferred $1,250,000 to the third-party entity. By so doing, the $1,000,000 of excess property would be nontaxable if it were not for the 2nd leg prohibition feature in Figure 9.6. In wealthy marital estates, Section 1041(a) is often used as an abusive tax shelter in the form of a family trust. It can shield taxable property transfers that were not intended to be shielded. Such an arrangement has all of the elements of a fraudulent transfer. Yet, no specific tax penalty is prescribed. The hope is that abusive transfers can be avoided by requiring mutual consent that only Section 1041 property is involved.

How One Court Ruled

Regulation § 1.1041-1T(c) Q/A-9 is tricky and frustrating. Even in nonabusive transfers of property, the regulatory intent is ambiguous. One of the first court cases to "test" its ambiguity is that of *Joann C. Arnes, CA-9, 93-1 USTC ¶ 50,016; 981 F2d 456.*

In the Arnes case, husband (John) and wife (Joann) owned co-equally 5,000 shares (at $1 per share) of a corporation franchise. They were divorced in 1988. At that time, the stock was worth $900,000 of which $450,000 belonged to Joann. The divorce agreement specified that Joann was to transfer her 2,500 shares to the corporation, and John, in turn, would pay Joann $450,000 (in installments over 10 years). Instead of John paying Joann, the corporation paid Joann.

On her 1988 income tax return, Joann reported $447,500 (450,000 − 2,500 basis) as long-term capital gain. Using the installment method, she computed and paid $53,053 in capital gains tax. In 1989, she realized that she had made a mistake (under Section 1041). She filed an amended return for 1988 claiming refund of the $53,053 amount. The IRS disallowed the refund claim. Joann then filed a petition for refund in the U.S. District Court. The district court disagreed with the IRS and ordered that the refund be paid.

The IRS appealed to the 9th Circuit Court of Appeals. Its rationale was that if neither Joann nor John is taxed, the $450,000 used to redeem Joann's share would be taken out of the corporation tax free.

The Appeals Court meticulously reviewed Section 1041(a) re "no gain or loss," etc. and Regulation § 1.1041-1T(c) Q/A-9 re "on behalf of," etc. The court concluded that—

A transfer was made "on behalf of" John Arnes if he received a benefit from the transfer. [He] did receive a benefit, because the transfer was part of the marital property settlement which settled any future community property claims that Joann Arnes could have asserted against John. . . . Joann is not required to recognize any gain on the transfer of her stock, because it is subject to Section 1041. The tax result is the same as if she had conveyed the property directly to John.

How Another Court Ruled

In another Section 1041 "on behalf of" case, the court ruled differently from that above. The published case is that of *Marsha Hatch Ingram, CA-9, 99-1 USTC ¶ 50,249*. The court ruled against the plaintiff (Marsha) by reasoning that Section 1041(a) did **not** apply. The transferred property was in reality a "sale."

When Marsha and Ken Hatch married in 1974, they purchased two lakefront lots (one with a home on it) and two roadside lots. They bought all four lots for $160,000. Of this amount, $100,000 (or 62.5%) was Marsha's separate property money, and $60,000 (or 37.5%) was Ken's separate property money.

The spouses divorced in February 1991. As part of their property settlement agreement, Marsha would get the two lakefront lots (including the family home). They both agreed that Ken would get the two roadside lots *plus* $400,000 from Marsha to equalize their community interest in the marital residence. No title changes to the property were made at divorce settlement time. Thus, all four lots remained in the names of Marsha and Ken as husband and wife (as co-owners).

In May 1991, all of the four lots were sold to the same buyer for $4,250,000. Of this amount $3,100,000 was paid to Marsha for "her" two lakefront lots. From this, she immediately paid to Ken the $400,000 that was due him. For "his" two roadside lots, Ken received $1,150,000.

Some 18 months later, the IRS audited Marsha's 1991 return and separately audited Ken's 1991 return. Since their divorce was final in 1991, each filed separately. The IRS held that Section 1041(a) and Regulation § 1.1041-1T(c) did NOT apply in this case. It construed the bulk sale as not being "incident to divorce." Thereupon, it assessed approximately $756,000 in tax against Marsha and approximately $417,000 in tax against Ken.

Under the IRS's threat of seizure of other assets, Marsha and Ken each paid the tax and each promptly filed claim for refund in the U.S. District Court. The District Court affirmed the tax assessment by the IRS. Marsha appealed to the 9th Circuit Court of Appeals (as cited above). Ken waited for the outcome of Marsha's appeal before filing his own appeal.

In substance, Marsha claimed that the entire sale qualified under Section 1041(a)(2) as being "incident to divorce." She reasoned that, because the divorce instrument required her to pay $400,000 to Ken, the entire sale was for the benefit of — or "on behalf of" — her obligation to Ken. Subsequently, the 9th Circuit affirmed the position of the District Court as well as the position of the IRS.

The 9th Circuit Court concluded that—

> Plainly, our "on behalf of" inquiry . . . turned on whether the plaintiff's transfer of property had relieved her former spouse of a specific legal obligation or liability . . . owed to her or to a third party. Because plaintiff's sale in this case did not satisfy any such obligation, the district court correctly held that she was not entitled to a tax refund under Section 1041(a)(2).

Marsha and Ken did not have an amicable divorce. They wrangled endlessly with each other. They quarreled over child support (they had three minor children), alimony payments, and property settlement terms. Their separate attorneys only made matters worse. The result was that the decree specified that Marsha was to be awarded the family residence until the children graduated from high school. In exchange for Marsha getting full ownership rights to the family home, she agreed to pay Ken $400,000.

As it turned out, all of the co-owned property (all four lots including the family home) were sold within three months after the divorce. The sale was necessitated by financial demands — mounting attorney fees, credit card debt, borrowed money, and rising living expenses. The property was not sold solely to pay off the $400,000 division-of-property obligation to Ken. Hence, Section 1041 did not apply.

As it also turned out, neither Marsha nor Ken — nor their attorneys — were aware of the impact of Section 1041 until the IRS started auditing each of their returns. As a consequence, the decree was not written with Section 1041 in mind. Had it been, the $400,000 to Ken in exchange for relinquishg his marital rights to the residence would have been a transfer incident to divorce. To identify the transfer more precisely, the residence should have been retitled in the name of Marsha only, subject to a $400,000 equalizing obligation to Ken.

Settlements Preceding Divorce

If you become annoyed with attorneys, but at least communicate with your separated spouse (before divorce is final), there is a special rule you should know about. It is called the "3-year rule" and addresses property settlements before divorce. It was enacted concurrently with Section 1041 and picks up on the thread of interspousal transfers being treated as nontaxable gifts.

This special rule is Section 2516: *Certain Property Settlements*. The term "certain" means those settlements which are negotiated before divorce is final and communicated to the IRS by filing a *U.S. Gift Tax Return*: Form 709. The "certain" also means with or without the role of attorneys, so long as the agreement is put in writing . . . and notarized. It then becomes a required attachment to the gift tax return.

Accordingly, Section 2516 reads in full as follows:

Where a husband and wife enter into a written agreement relative to their marital and property rights and divorce occurs within the 3-year period beginning on the date 1 year before such agreement is entered into (whether or not such agreement is approved by the divorce decree), any transfers of property or interests in property made pursuant to such agreement—

(1)   to either spouse in settlement of his or her marital or property rights, or
(2)   to provide a reasonable allowance for the support of issue of the marriage during minority,

shall be deemed to be transfers made for a full and adequate consideration in money or money's worth.

The phrase "full and adequate consideration" is tax jargon meaning: no gain, no loss on the property transactions. This is another way of saying that the transfers are nontaxable, if consummated within three years before the final decree. As depicted in Figure 9.7, this should be a worthwhile inducement to both spouses.

Regulation § 25.6019-3(b): *Disclosure of Section 2516 transfers* requires that—

The transfer [of marital property] *must be disclosed by the transferor upon a gift tax return for the calendar year in which the* [property settlement] *agreement becomes effective, and a copy of the agreement must be attached to the return. In addition, a certified copy of the final divorce decree shall be furnished the* [IRS] *. . . not later than 60 days after the divorce is granted.*

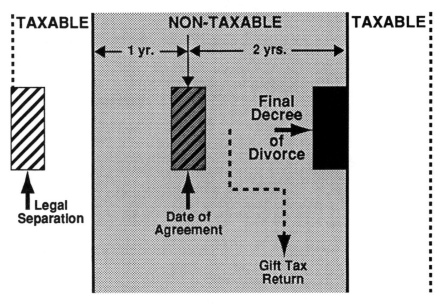

Fig. 9.7 - The 3-Year (No Tax) Rule for Marital Property Transfers

Why a gift tax return?

Because its Schedule A thereon requires that the transferor spouse (under penalties of perjury) state his/her "adjusted (tax) basis" in the property transferred. The tax importance of basis transfer is too frequently overlooked by divorce attorneys during the heat of their legal exchanges. Hence, the Internal Revenue Code enables communicative spouses to resolve their own property settlement issues. They can . . . but will they?

10

TRANSFEREE BURDENS

Under Section 1041, The Transferee (Recipient) Of Property Has The Sole Burden For All Tax Accounting, Long After Divorce Is Final. Such Is The Consequence Of The "Carryover Basis" Rule. Transferor Spouses Are Seldom Cooperative, Preferring Instead To Seek Bankruptcy Protection, Overload The Property With Debt, Or Brazenly Overvalue It For Faster Divorce Settlement Writeoffs. To Counter These Tactics, The Transferee Must Make Probing Inquiries Before Accepting Any Property Offerings. The Clear PROPERTY OF CHOICE Is The Marital Residence. When Sold, A $250,000 Capital Gain Exclusion Applies.

As was evident in the two court cases cited in Chapter 9, property settlement issues can become contentious and prolonged. There are disputes between the spouses, and between the spouses' attorneys. The process — in and out of court — can go on for six years and still be treated as transfers of property incident to divorce. In those cases where substantial-value properties are at issue (i.e., settlements over $1,000,000), the litigation can go on for more than six years.

As also indicated in Chapter 9 (Figure 9.5 particularly), the fundamental property settlement tax rule is Section 1041. The substance of this rule is that there shall be "no gain or loss" on the transfer of *property* between spouses (or former spouses). That is, there is no income tax consequence to the transferor spouse: the one giving up property. Nor is there any income tax consequence to the transferee spouse: the one receiving property. This no-tax feature enables the parties to concentrate on making the division of properties more equitable between themselves.

What happens after the divorce is final, and a property item is sold or exchanged to a third party? At such point in time, there **are** tax consequences. Any gain or loss is tax recognized depending on the nature and use of the property at the time of its disposition.

To understand what the downstream tax consequences may be, the *transferee burden* rule comes into play. This rule establishes the tax basis in the disposed-of property. The particular rule is subsection (b) of Section 1041. Its full title is: ***Transfer Treated as Gift; Transferee has Transferor's Basis.***

In this chapter, therefore, we want to explore the transferee-burden rule quite thoroughly. We also want to point out its pitfalls and suggest what to do to alleviate the downstream inequities that will arise. No tax law is all perfect; subsection 1041(b) is no exception.

Text of Section 1041(b)

The full text of Section 1041(b) reads as follows—

*In the case of **any property** described in subsection (a)* [No gain or loss, etc.]—

> *(1) for the purpose of this subtitle* [Subtitle A: Income Taxes]*, the property shall be treated as **acquired** by the transferee **by gift**, and*
> *(2) **the basis of the transferee** in the property **shall be** the adjusted basis of the transferor.* [Emphasis added.]

Note, first off, the reference to *any property*. This raises the question: What kind of property are they talking about? Keep in mind that we are dealing with incident-to-divorce property only.

The answer is: ***Any kind*** of property which has a market value of some determinable amount. Although the regulations do not identify a specific amount, the general practice is to consider only those items which have fair market value (at time of transfer) of

$1,000 or more. If some such realistic floor were not set, every pair of old shoes and every stick of old furniture that changed hands incident to divorce would have to be market appraised. This $1,000 value level is our rule-of-thumb only. It is not beyond challenge. However, in a $1,000,000 plus marital estate, items of less than $1,000 are at "noise level."

"Any kind" of property means real estate, tangible items, intangible assets, and personal effects. Real property consists of land, improvements to land, structures on land, and natural resources. Tangible property consists of vehicles, machinery, equipment, tools, antiques, collectibles (guns, clocks, stamps, coins, paintings), and valued jewelry and furs. Intangible property consists of stocks, bonds, pensions, annuities, securities, mutual funds, trust deeds, certificates of deposit, savings accounts, checking accounts, "greenbacks," and other paper assets. Personal effects are clothing, inexpensive jewelry, household furniture and furnishings, sport equipment, handicraft, memorabilia, and other purely personal-use items. Any of these and other similar items constitute "property" if, separately, it has a market value of $1,000 or more.

Furthermore, the eligible property must be that which is . . . *described in subsection (a)* [of Section 1041]. Actually, no physical description of property of any kind is given in subsection (a). Thus, the "applicable property" is that which is transferred . . . *from an individual to (or in trust for the benefit of) . . . a spouse or former spouse.* Hence, property distributions from ordinary trusts, from partnerships, associations, or corporations do NOT qualify. Such are entities; not spousal individuals.

The Mandate: Basis Carryover

Section 1041(b) establishes two tax characterizing features. The first feature is that the transferred property is treated as acquired by gift. That is, it was not purchased; it was not exchanged; it was not found. This means that the acquirer (the transferee spouse) gets no adjustment to the amount of capital invested in the property for any cash or other item of property given up, or for any debt assumed, to acquire the gifted property. In other words, it is a pure gift with no out-of-pocket consideration by the transferee factored in.

The second feature of the transferee-acquired property is that it takes on the tax basis of the transferor. This is so mandated by paragraph (2) of subsection 1041(b). The mandatory aspect reads—

*The basis of the transferee in the property **shall be** the adjusted basis of the transferor.*

That is, the transferred property carries with it the basis burden of the transferor. The acquirer/transferee has no choice in the matter. This is known as the "basis carryover" doctrine of divorce-acquired property. The principle involved is depicted in Figure 10.1.

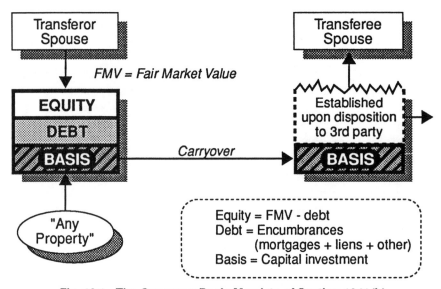

Fig. 10.1 - The Carryover Basis Mandate of Section 1041(b)

To amplify the above (and Figure 10.1), it is instructive to cite Regulation 1.1041-1T(d)(A-11). This regulation reads—

*In all cases, the basis of the transferred property in the hands of the transferee is the adjusted basis of such property in the hands of the transferor immediately before the transfer. Even if the transfer is a bona fide sale, the transferee does not acquire a basis in the transferred property equal to the transferee's cost (the fair market value). **The carryover basis rule applies*** *whether the adjusted basis of the transferred property is less than, equal to, or greater than its fair market value at the time of the transfer (or the value of any consideration provided by the transferee) and applies for purposes of determining loss as well as gain upon the subsequent disposition of the property by the transferee.* [Emphasis added.]

What does this regulation mean?

First of all, it opens up a whole Pandora's box of tax traps for the transferee. Traditionally, property settlements have been negotiated in terms of swapping property rights that are equal in value, equitable in value, or based on some markup or discount in value. The negotiating process is now complicated by the carryover-basis rule. We say "complicated" because most divorcing spouses understand "market value"; very few understand "basis carryover."

Transferor's "Basis" Explained

The term *basis* is a tax accounting reference. It is a dollar amount with respect to which gain or loss is computed, when property is sold or transferred to a nonrelated party. It is the amount of capital (money) invested in property.

One's capital basis in property usually is quite different from the market's value of that property. Basis — more properly: *adjusted basis* — is one's total investment in property, from date of acquisition to date of disposition. Acquisition basis and disposition basis may — and often do — differ. Hence, the term "adjusted" basis. There are plus adjustments (additions) to and minus adjustments (subtractions) from, the acquisition basis.

Market value, on the other hand, is the retail price that an item of property would bring, if offered to the general public. The market value may be greater than, less than, or equal to one's basis in property.

A simple, diagrammatic visualization of basis versus value is presented in Figure 10.2.

Suppose, for example, one paid $10,000 (basis) to acquire an item of property, say x shares of stock Y. A few years later,

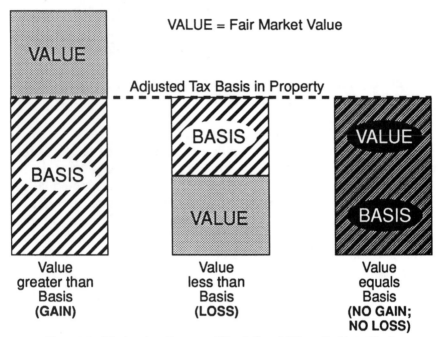

Fig. 10.2 - Distinction Between "Basis" and "Value" (Simplified)

suppose its market value is $15,000. If the property is sold at market value (to an unrelated party), there would be a $5,000 gain. *Any gain* on the downstream sale of property acquired by divorce is *always taxable.* Except for the marital residence, which enjoys a special exclusion of gain, there is no way out!

Suppose, now, the $10,000 (basis) property had a market value of $5,000. If sold at the market value, there would be a $5,000 loss. Losses from subsequent disposition of divorce-acquired property may, may not, or may partially be tax recognized. It all depends on the nature and use of the property in the hands of the transferee when it is sold. If property is used primarily for personal purposes, the loss is not tax recognized. If used in a trade or business, the loss is fully recognized. If held primarily for investment, the loss is partially recognized. It is recognized only to the extent of $3,000 of net capital loss for any taxable year.

Suppose, again, that the $10,000 (basis) property had a market value also of $10,000. If sold (after the divorce) for $10,000 there would be zero gain and zero loss. Only in this case, then, would divorce-acquired property be truly tax free.

This brings us again to the point that we were trying to make previously. Property acquired incident to divorce is nontaxable . . . *only at that time*! Nontaxable means tax free only in those few instances when the transferee's basis in the property exactly equals the market value of that property. In all other situations, nontaxable means *tax deferred* when market value exceeds basis (that is, when a gain) and *tax accountable* when market value is less than basis (that is, when a loss). Gains are always taxable, whereas losses are generally limited.

Now the poignant point.

What happens if a transferee's basis in property cannot be resurrected when an item of property is sold, several years after the final decree of divorce?

Answer: If a transferee spouse cannot prove convincingly his or her tax basis in property sold, the IRS arbitrarily assigns *zero basis*. From a zero tax reference, any market value is all gain: fully taxable. From a zero reference, there can be no loss whatsoever. There is no assignment of negative basis for below zero.

Do you sense now the tax importance of knowing your "adjusted basis" in property acquired incident to divorce?

Transferor's Obligation (Supposedly)

What is the property settlement tax concern to which we have been alluding? Where is the tax catch?

There are tax burdens downstream. The after-divorce taxes are payable solely by the transferee. The amount of tax is determined from basis information supposedly supplied by the transferor. Let us explain.

There are two sets of regulations on which we want to brief you. These two are:

Reg. 1.1041-1T(d): Tax Consequences of Transfers Subject to Section 1041

Reg. 1.1041-1T(e): Notice and Recordkeeping Requirement with Respect to Section 1041

With regard to the **transferor**, subregulation (d)(A-10) states in significant part that—

The transferor of property under section 1041 recognizes no gain or loss on the transfer even if the transfer was in exchange for the release of marital rights or other consideration. This rule applies regardless of whether the transfer is of property separately owned by the transferor or is a division (equal or unequal) of community property.

At first reading, it appears that the transferor is free and clear of all tax obligations. He merely quit-claims, signs off, and turns over the agreed property item (or items) to the transferee. Does he then simply walk away?

Answer: He probably will. But he is not supposed to. He has a records obligation to the transferee.

The transferor's obligation is set forth in subregulation (e)(A-14). There, it states that—

*A transferor of property under section 1041 **must**, at the time of the transfer, **supply the transferee with records** sufficient to determine the adjusted basis and holding period of the property as of the date of the transfer. Such records must [then] be preserved and kept accessible by the **transferee**.* [Emphasis added.]

Regulation 1.041-1T(e)(A-14) seems pretty clear. It says: *A transferor of property MUST supply the transferee with records.* Hence, before walking away from a property settlement, the transferor spouse is supposed to supply to the transferee sufficient records to establish the transferor's adjusted basis in the property.

What happens if the transferor refuses, or, as is more likely, doesn't have any tax records to turn over to the transferee? There are no tax penalties that punish the transferor for not complying with subregulation (e)(A-14). And this is the injustice of it all.

When asked for basis records, many a transferor spouse is going to say to the transferee spouse: "Don't hassle me for the tax records. If you want the property, take it; if you don't want the property, don't take it. I don't want to be bothered with your downstream tax problems."

Example: No Basis Records

Trying to acquire basis records for post-divorce property sales is generally an exercise in futility. Here's a recent example on point.

As part of a several-million-dollar property settlement, the wife received a 5-acre tract of desert land in the southeastern corner of California. The husband, a high-stakes real estate attorney, acquired the land in 1986. He acquired it in a nontaxable exchange (IRC Section 1031) with other real estate properties he had held. As "boot" (other than cash or property), he forgave all legal fees due him by the former landowner(s). No creditable basis records were kept; the true market value of the land was never professionally appraised. Based on his "superior knowledge" in the real estate world, the husband asserted that the property was worth at least $265,000. This apparently satisfied the divorce court.

In 1993, the property settlement order read (in part)—

Respondent [the husband] *shall have credited to him on the judgment any amounts paid to Petitioner* [the wife] *as follows:*

(1) . . .

(2) $265,000 **when title** *to the five (+ or -) acres of land in* _____, *California* **is obtained by Petitioner** *free and clear of liens and claims; and*

(3) . . .   [Emphasis added.]

Title to the land was transferred to the wife in late 1994. It was **not** "free and clear of lines and claims," as the court had ordered. In late 1998, the wife received from the County Tax Collector a **Defaulted Property Tax Statement**. The amount of delinquent taxes on the land was $30,254. The statement also included a bold-imprinted notice: TAX SALE on February 24, 1999. [A "tax sale" is the public auction of real estate for the recovery of delinquent taxes, penalties, interest, and other claims.]

Hoping to avoid the tax sale, the wife listed the property for sale through a licensed real estate broker in the situs area of the desert land. In late 1998, the property sold for $100,000. Taken from this amount were: sales commission $9,500; delinquent taxes $30,254; and closing costs of $1,145 (total $40,949). The wife net received $59,051 on the deal (100,000 – 40,949).

The husband claimed $265,000 credit against his property settlement. This despite the fact that the net proceeds from the post-divorce sale amounted to only $59,051. Through her attorney and the husband's attorney, the wife requested the husband's tax basis records on the desert land. She also requested the husband's credit on his property settlement obligation be reduced from $265,000 to $59,051. The husband adamantly refused to honor either of the two requests. He (an attorney) put out the word: "Let her sue me if she wants to do so."

In January 1999, the former wife did indeed sue her former husband. Her primary allegation was that the husband had defaulted on the property settlement order. The land was conveyed to her heavily encumbered with delinquent tax liens . . . instead of being free and clear of those liens. On March 20, 2000, the court ruled against the wife. It did not address her request for basis records. On the default issue, the court concluded—

That petitioner [wife] *has failed in her burden of proof that Respondent* [husband] *is in default of any orders of this court.*

In a situation like this, what does the wife do? Under Regulation 1.1041-1T(e)(A-14), the husband was *supposed* to convey to the wife all basis records in connection with his acquisition of the 5-acre parcel of land. He had no intention of ever doing so . . . the IRS notwithstanding.

Later, the wife found out that in his legal practice, the husband frequently sought to couch his legal fees into the exchange language of Section 1031: *Nontaxble Exchange of Property Held for Productive Use or Investment.* Doing so meant that he would pay a capital gains rate of 20% instead of 55% (the combined income, social security, and medicare tax rates). The wife also found out that his regular billing fee was $265 per hour. The coincidence of the

$265 per hour and the $265,000 land value asserted by the husband was just too uncanny. It then dawned on the wife that the husband had charged off 1,000 hours of legal services to his various property exchanges. (Tax accountingwise, it is improper to do this.) Thereupon, the wife concluded that the $265,000 was indeed the husband's tax basis in the five acres of desert land.

No Basis; No Section 1041

A common problem in many divorce cases is that the impact of Section 1041 is neither mentioned nor referenced in the final decree. Nor is there any mention of the basis carryover rule on property transfers. Oversight of these matters can lead to serious tax trauma to one spouse or the other. A particular case on this point is: *Susan T. Martin, 97-2 USTC ¶ 50,731.* At stake was the taxability of the wife's $5,750,000 share of community property interests.

Susan and Ken Martin had been married 33 years. They were legally separated in 1990 and were final divorced in 1991. The property settlement portion of the decree addressed only the regular marital items. It was totally silent with respect to Section 1041 and tax basis matters.

In early 1991 (before the final), Ken filed for bankruptcy protection. He listed his assets as being zero. Suspecting that Ken had hidden assets somewhere, Susan pursued legal discovery. It turned out that Ken had a Gas Purchase Contract with Tenneco Gas Louisiana, Inc. ("Tenneco"). The contract had no specific face value. It was the right to purchase very large quantities of gas at a fixed price, which, at the time, was about one-fourth the current (1993) market value of gas. This cost differential made the contract a very valuable asset. It later turned out the contract was worth nearly $13,000,000 (13 million).

Upon learning of its value, Susan contacted Tenneco. She offered to sell to Tenneco her one-half community interest in the gas purchase contract. Tenneco offered Susan $5,750,000 for her rights thereto. She accepted Tenneco's offer in mid-1993 and subsequently received the full amount.

Susan filed her 1993 income tax return in a timely manner. She attached Form 8275: *Disclosure Statement.* She took the position that the entire amount was nontaxable pursuant to Section 1041: *Transfers of Property Incident to Divorce*. The IRS disagreed with Susan's reliance on Section 1041. In early 1996, Susan paid the tax (nearly $1,150,000!) and thereupon immediately filed claim for refund in the U.S. District Court.

In mid-1997, the District Court ruled against Susan Martin. Among other statements by the court, its conclusion was:

> Susan cannot escape the fact that she received $5.75 million from Tenneco for the sale of her claims against Ken Martin's 1991 Bankruptcy Estate. . . . Further, . . . she must recognize gain unless her basis in the claims was equal to or greater than the amount she received. However, because her claims against the bankruptcy estate had no basis, she must pay tax on the **entire** $5.75 million received from Tenneco.

Shortly thereafter, Susan appealed the District Court's decision to the U.S. Court of Appeals, 5th Circuit [98-2 USTC ¶ 50,889]. In late 1998, the Appeals Court ruled:

> The district court did not err in holding the entire $5.75 million taxable and denying Susan's claim for a refund of the taxes she paid on the transaction.

Critique of "Susan" Case

The litigative aspects of the Susan T. Martin case above extended over a period of **eight years**! This is the period from August 1990 (date of legal separation) through November 1998 (final decision by the Court of Appeals). Can you not imagine the exorbitant legal fees involved?

What were the factors causing so much time and cost?

The key factor, we think, is that the property settlement arrangement made no reference whatsoever to Section 1041. Even the briefest mention of this section would have been helpful. The idea is to express the intent of both parties to conform any property transfers to the "No gain, No loss" aspects of Section 1041(a). The compliance language should be expressive enough to cover all community property interests that may be discovered later (such as the $13,000,000 gas purchase contract).

Any reference to Section 1041 and the designation of properties therewith should establish an *obligation* of one spouse to convey property to the other spouse. Had this been done, Susan's 1/2 community property interest in the gas purchase contract would have been conveyed **from** the bankruptcy estate. Wisely, as it turned out, Susan did not join with Ken in the petition for bankruptcy. Ken, therefore, was the only debtor of that estate. As a debtor with a property transfer obligation to Susan, Section 1041 would have applied as legislatively intended. Instead of no tax, Susan paid (approximately) $1,150,000 in capital gains tax.

There is a fundamental reason why Susan's receipt of $5,750,000 was taxable. She negotiated directly with Tenneco, Inc. instead of with the bankruptcy estate. Tenneco had no Section 1041 obligation to Susan. The transaction, therefore, was an outright sale to a third party (not incident to divorce). Tenneco, being the guarantor of the contract, wanted simply to protect its interests. A depiction of what we see as having taken place is presented in Figure 10.3.

Subsequent to buying out Susan's interest, Tenneco bought out Ken's interest in the contract. It paid Ken's bankruptcy estate $7,000,000. Thus, Ken was quite solvent; he was not bankrupt at all. The bankruptcy effort was a sham. Its sole purpose was to conceal from Susan what Ken's real assets were

It is almost common practice these days for well-to-do transferors to threaten bankruptcy when going through divorce. Our position is: Let the threatening spouse go ahead and file for bankruptcy. By doing so, all debtor assets come under the custody and supervision of the Trustee of the Bankruptcy Estate. The trustee has a fiduciary duty to disclose to bona fide creditors and claimants the extent to which their Proofs of Claims are covered. Dealing with a trustee is more business-like than dealing with an embittered spouse who is trying to hide major assets.

Vigilance by Transferee

There are other things that transferors do (besides filing for bankruptcy) to thwart the expectations of their transferees. A common tactic is to load the property (intended for the transferee)

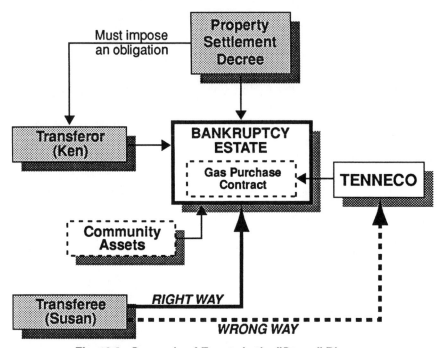

Fig. 10.3 - Synopsis of Events in the "Susan" Divorce

with additional mortgage debt, creditor liens, and other encumbrances (tax delinquencies, etc.). When the property is actually conveyed to the transferee, its equity (FMV minus debt) is minimal. In order to clear title to the property, the transferee has to agree to assume responsibility for all debts and encumbrances on it. Thus, downstream, when the property is sold, the transferee not only has to pay the capital gains tax, he/she has also to pay off all encumbrances as well as all selling costs. The result is that very little net cash accrues to the seller.

To illustrate the debt overload tactic, consider that the property intended for transfer to the other spouse is valued at $100,000. The transferor's tax basis (capital investment) in the property is $15,000. Thus, the transferor has an $85,000 equity in the property (100,000 – 15,000). He borrows $65,000 against his equity by using the property as security. The property is title-conveyed to the transferee spouse. A year or two later, the transferee sells the property for

$100,000 (assume selling costs of $5,000). How much cash will the transferee realize from the deal?

First, the gross proceeds from the sale is $95,000 (100,000 – 5,000). Next, the $65,000 mortgage debt has to be paid off. The available cash left is now $30,000 (95,000 – 65,000). There is an $80,000 capital gain (95,000 – basis) on which tax has to be paid. This tax is $16,000 (80,000 x 20%) federal **plus** approximately $4,000 (80,000 x 5%) state. The bottom line is that the transferee/seller sees only $10,000 out of the deal (30,000 – 16,000 – 4,000).

In contrast, the transferor gets a "credit" of $100,000 against his property settlement decree. Still further, he gets $65,000 cash (the mortgage money) on which he pays no tax whatsoever . . . as per Section 1041(a).

Not a very fair deal for the transferee spouse, is it? Do you see what we are driving at? The transferee spouse has to "think downtream" before agreeing to property settlement terms. He/she has to be vigilant — and insistent — on knowing the **equity value** of the property being transferred. Market value and tax basis relate primarily to the tax imposed on a downstream sale. They tell you very little about the downstream cash proceeds.

Every divorce situation will have its own set of fairness concerns. Resolving these concerns requires that the transferee spouse make **probing inquiries** into the properties that he/she will receive from the other spouse. Such a task will not be easy; the legal and emotional wrangling will be disruptive. Nevertheless, some suggestions in this regard are presented in Figure 10.4. The main target in Figure 10.4 is *investment-type* properties. These are properties which are likely to be sold downstream for capital gain or capital loss tax recognition purposes. Other than the marital residence, purely personal-use property (cars, boats, furniture, fixtures, etc.) will require no downstream tax accounting.

Demand Gift Tax Return

Face it. Despite what we urge in Figure 10.4, rarely will a transferor spouse, or his/her attorney, willingly comply with your requests. You know what the routine will be. He or she will play hardball to thwart your every move. But, since you are the ultimate

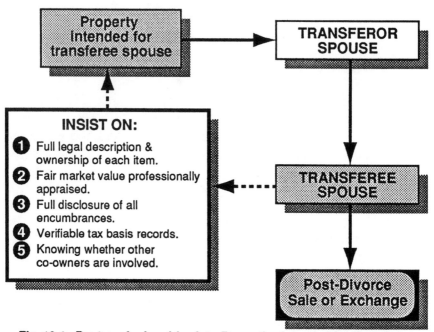

Fig. 10.4 - Pre-transfer Inquiries Into Properties Intended for Transferee

tax obligee to the IRS, you've got to get rough. Now's the time to pull that ace out of your sleeve. Demand a gift tax return!

We've already explained that interspousal property transfers are treated as nontaxable gifts. Such treatment, however, does NOT exonerate the transferor from compliance with Regulation § 1.1041-1T(e)(A-14): *Notice and recordkeeping requirement with respect to transactions under Section 1041* [Basis records]. Nor does such treatment exonerate the transferor from compliance with Regulation § 25.6019-3(d): *Disclosure of transfers coming within provisions of Section 2516* [Gift tax returns].

Therefore, our suggestion is this. Demand from the transferor that he/she prepare Form 709: *U.S. Gift Tax Return* by completing Schedule A thereon: *Computation of Taxable Gifts*. This schedule requires documented information in the following columnar form:

Col. A — Item number
Col. B — Description of gift
Col. C — Adjusted basis of gift

Col. D — Date of gift
Col. E — Value at date of gift

In the computation portion, there is a special line entry:

Gifts of interests to spouse for which a marital deduction will be claimed, based on items _____ of Schedule A.

The implication here is that if the marital deduction is not claimed by the transferor spouse (under Sections 1041 and/or 2516), the transferor himself/herself will have a **gift tax** to pay. Make this point clear in your demand communication. Also make clear that if no meaningful response is received, you will attach a copy of your demand notice to Form 8275: *Disclosure Statement*, which you will attach to your next Form 1040 filed with the IRS. This procedure generally will induce the IRS to **audit** the transferor's own Form 1040. Once the transferor goes through the IRS audit wringer, he/she may thereafter be more cooperative.

The Marital Residence

The property of choice for a transferee spouse is the marital residence. It is so because it is the only significant personal-use property item that has the potential to appreciate in value over time. This makes the marital residence a good investment as well as a place of abode.

There are other advantages to the transferee spouse receiving full ownership of the marital residence. The most noteworthy are:

1. Tax basis records are more readily available, or more readily determinable. The transferee spouse (being part owner) already has access to (or physical possession of) most of the information needed.

2. Encumbrances on the property (mortgages, debts, and liens) are more readily ascertainable. Inquiries to the county recorder's office (where legal title and encumbrances are recorded) are amicably processed.

3. Realistic appraisals of the fair market value of the residence can be independently obtained. This can be done via comparable neighborhood sales without undue influence or distortion by the transferor spouse.

4. After the transferor spouse moves out of the marital residence, the transferee spouse gets a separate $250,000 *exclusion of gain* should it be sold after occupying it for more than two years [Section 121(a), (b)].

Property ownership and marital rights are a function of state law: not federal law. Accordingly, the marital residence just before divorce may be 50/50 owned (by husband and wife) or non-50/50 owned. Depending on the state of residence, 50/50 ownership means either joint tenancy, tenants-by-the-entirety, or community property. Non-50/50 ownership means tenants-in-common. Such ownership may be 35/65, 75/25 . . . or some other non-equal ownership split. Upon agreement by both spouses, either voluntarily or judicially imposed, the move-out spouse (transferor) has to convey clear title to the stay-in (transferee) spouse. This is done via a *quitclaim deed* or other legal conveyance document.

When a marital residence is co-owned by husband and wife, there are **two** transferor-transferee situations. To illustrate the point, assume the residence is 65% owned by the husband and 35% owned by the wife (a 65/35 split). Assume further that the husband is the move-out (transferor) and the wife is the stay-in (transferee). Two reciprocal legal conveyances are required, namely:

[1] Transferor (husband) quitclaims 65% of his marital residence interests to transferee (wife).

[2] Transferor (wife) quitclaims an equivalent amount of other marital property interests to transferee (husband).

The above is the fundamental premise upon which the Section 1041(a) "no gain/no loss" rule applies. **Afterwards,** and after the divorce is final, each transferee is responsible for his or her own tax accounting burdens.

11

FOLLOWUP MATTERS

Within 60 Days After Divorce, One Should Review Diligently His/Her Legal Obligations And Tax Affairs. For This, A Court-Certified Copy Of The FINAL DECREE And Its Attachments Is Required. As To Matters Of Head Of Household Status, Dependency Exemptions, Alimony "Paid" And Alimony "Received," "Split Sale" Of The Marital Residence, And Any Co-Ownership Of Rental Property, There Is Some Likelihood Of An IRS AUDIT. Irritating Computer Demands Can Develop Unless Bankers, Brokers, Payers, And Tax Shelter Managers Are Notified Of Correct SSNs And Address Changes.

The concluding act in divorce proceedngs is a Final Judgment of Dissolution of Marriage. It might also be a final judgment of legal separation or nullity. The net effect is the same. Two persons, man and woman, holding themselves out as husband and wife, are no longer such.

The closing words in the judgment decree are along the following lines:

THE COURT ORDERS—
That a final judgment of dissolution of marriage be entered, and that all provisions of the _____ decree, except as otherwise attached, be made binding the same as if set forth in full, and that the parties be restored to the status of unmarried persons.

The order is signed and dated by the Judge of the Superior Court or the Magistrate having jurisdiction over family law matters. The clerk of the court takes possession of the original and makes certified copies upon request. This order is followed by a Notice of Entry of Judgment showing the date, book, and page number of entry into Official Records of the county of jurisdiction.

The exact wordings and procedures will vary in different states, different courts, and with different attorneys involved. But the general idea is the same. There is a recorded legal document terminating the marital estate.

At this point, the divorce is final in all legal respects. However, it is *not* final in all tax respects. There are many remaining tax matters to be cleared up. While one's legal status will be restored to that of a single person, his tax status will be more complicated than before his marriage. Clearing up and refocusing one's tax affairs is what this chapter is all about.

Immediate Post-Divorce Review

Going through divorce can be an exhausting experience, emotionally and financially. When the final is granted there is a temporary sense of relief. A "little celebration" may be held. There is a feeling that all is behind one, and that the time has come to take on a new life style. In this frame of mind, many tax mistakes can be made. The IRS can be unforgiving on divorce mistakes.

After the temporary relief has worn off, it is necessary to get down to the important business of tax reorientation. The first step in this regard is to get a *certified copy* of the final judgment and its referenced attachments. This will cost a small fee, payable to the county clerk. You want the officially recorded document: not the working copies that your attorney may have furnished you. Judicially recorded documents must have all applicable blank spaces filled in. Such documents often have handwritten notes, corrections, and other markings (such as, "Endorsed-Filed") which are official. You want in your own hands the true final court order.

With a certified copy of your final divorce decree and attachments in hand, your next step is to review it thoroughly. Read it and re-read it. Particularly note any ongoing legal obligations that you might have. Typical such obligations are payments to former spouse, payments against marital debts, completion of property transfers and retitling certain properties, warranties against incurring post-divorce debts assignable to former spouse, and so on. Do not try to be vindictive or try to get even. Do what is right. Do what you are court-ordered to do, even though your former spouse may not do likewise.

Next photocopy the final decree and attachments, and take it to a tax person. Have him review the final terms cold. Have him point out to you your tax benefits and your tax burdens. Have him outline a worksheet for preparing your upcoming tax return. He may point out serious tax omissions in the final decree. If such omissions exist — rarely do they not — he may suggest ways to cover yourself in the event of a tax audit.

For example, suppose you are required to pay alimony and child support monthly. A tax person would urge you to make payments on separate personal checks: one check for alimony, one check for child support (each month). Mark each check "alimony" or "child support" as appropriate. Be sure to date each check correctly. Then start a separate tax file for each category of payment. Include in each file your canceled checks, chronologically arranged.

The best tax proof of meeting your alimony and child support obligations are your *canceled checks*. In this high-tech era of credit cards, sweep accounts, personal computers, e-mail, and electronic bank transfers, the writing of personal checks is tabbed as old fashioned. Nevertheless, when the tax audit comes, there is no simpler, more direct, and more convincing evidence of payment than canceled checks. So, be old fashioned . . . and be tax wise.

Likelihood of IRS Audit

This being a tax book, our position is that no divorce is truly final until each spouse has gone through the audit wringer. Officially, a tax audit is called an "examination." But it is more than this. It is an after-the-fact process of forcing more revenue into the U.S. Treasury. IRS experience has shown that divorced taxpayers are a lucrative source of additional tax, for very little effort being expended by its agents.

When divorce matters are at issue, audit probing becomes painful and delays become protracted. It is as though the government were reopening the entire divorce proceeding to extract every ounce of revenue blood that it can.

Ordinary audit issues are magnified in cases of divorce. This is because, invariably, divorcing spouses take opposite positions on a tax issue. One spouse tries to use the IRS as a club-of-revenge against the other spouse. As a result, the IRS is bound to win against one spouse or the other. And, often, it wins against both.

If one former spouse is audited, it does not necessarily follow that the other spouse also will be audited. If the spouse first to be audited "passes muster," the second audit is unlikely. This suggests that, during the years of separation and divorce, the parties should try to cooperate on tax issues, and resolve them, if at all possible. If not possible, the more diligent spouse should prepare for audit.

What is the likelihood of your post-divorce return being audited?

As a divorcee, we think the likelihood is at least 10% or more. If you are a "high profile" divorcee (where monetary settlements exceed $1,000,000), the likelihood jumps to 30% or more. By contrast, if you were an ordinary filer not going through divorce, the likelihood of audit would be 1% or less.

What makes divorce returns so susceptible to IRS audits?

Short answer: The crossing-up of social security numbers on ex-spousal returns accompanied by inconsistent matching entries. The longer answer: Where matters of child support, alimony payments, and property settlement (involving businesses, investments, and pension plans) drag on for years, tax conflicts are bound to arise. Tax conflicts between former spouses rarely avoid IRS audits.

How easy is it for the IRS's computer to spot tax conflicts between former spouses who are filing totally separate returns?

Answer: Quite easy. For example, you claim one child as a dependent. To claim so, you must give that child's full name, social security number, and relationship. Suppose your former spouse also claims the same child. Bingo! Another "for example": You claim $50,000 as deductible alimony and list your former spouse's social security number. Your former spouse reports only $20,000 "Alimony received." Another Bingo!

Head of Household Status

The Master Computer is programmed to detect various signals from entries on a return, via checkboxes, line numbers, and data processing sequences. There is no need ever to have a specific question on a return: "Is divorce in process (initiated, pending, final) during the taxable year?" The computer can spot the telltale indications instantly.

One of the first telltale signs is the filing status checkbox: Head of household. If there is a check mark in this box, following a year in which there was a joint Form 1040, there is probability of an audit, or at least a questionnaire being sent.

The head of household checkbox instruction looks like this:

☐ *Head of household (with qualifying person). If the qualifying person is your child but not your dependent, enter child's name here* _____.

If this box is checked on your 1040, the computer scanner is looking for a child's name *either* in the adjacent space OR in the exemption space provided for dependent children.

If the same child's name appears in the head of household space *and* in the dependent children's space, you will be questioned. Count on it. The IRS will send you Form 4752: *Questionnaire — Head of Household.* You will be asked about your marital status and whether the named child lived with you all year. There will be various other questions and checkboxes. You will be asked to itemize the total cost of keeping up your home, and what portion you paid. If you received child support, you will be asked how much and who paid for it.

If you respond properly to Form 4752, that may end it. If not, audit — eventually — will ensue.

At audit you will be asked to provide a certified copy of such documents as:

Child Custody Order
Child Support Order
Legal Separation Order

Final Divorce Decree

Hopefully, you will have these documents available. If not, the auditor senses a kill and will instantly open up other tax wounds.

You will be asked to produce records proving all household costs, such as—

Rent	Utilities
Mortgage interest	Home repairs
Property taxes	Domestic help
Home insurance	Food eaten in home

A *household cost diary* would be an ideal way to establish your total costs. From this total, any court-ordered child support payments would be subtracted, to see if you paid more than 50% of the household costs. The term "child support" means just that: support of the child, not of the household.

A *child custody diary* (for each child) is essential where your full-year custody is questioned. All nights away from home should be recorded. Notations should be made indicating where the child stayed, the name of the person in charge, and the reason for being away. Acceptable reasons are vacation, schools, visitation with other parent (or with grandparents), hospital stay by custodial parent, or out-of-town business trip by custodial parent.

What an auditor is looking for is that you have full custodial control for the greater portion of the year. Ordinarily, this means more than six months, even though there were short periods of reasonable absence during the year.

A federal problem arises where there are 50/50 joint custody arrangements under state family law (California, for example). Unless the parents have an alternate-year understanding with each other whereby parent A can claim more than 50% custody in one year and parent B more than 50% custody the next year, neither would be able to claim head of household.

Most head of household taxpayers lose on this audit issue because they do not keep adequate records and diaries. Whenever it can, the goal of the IRS is to deny head of household status and any child-dependency exemption. Single status is assigned with one exemption (for yourself). This will cause you additional tax. It will also cost penalty and interest on the additional tax.

Claiming Dependency Exemptions

If the custodial parent releases claim to the child exemption, and consents so in writing (by signing For 8332), the noncustodial parent may claim the exemption. You can be sure the IRS is going to check this matter very closely on each parent's Form 1040. Computer cross-checking is automatic on these matters.

Most persons who have ever filed a Form 1040 tax return know that it contains some checkboxes for entering the number of exemptions claimed. The information is entered on the front of the form, about one-third of the way down from the top. The checkboxes are inside a full-width block labeled: EXEMPTIONS.

The very first checkbox is labeled "Yourself." Obviously you always check this box. The second checkbox is labeled "Spouse." You must be very careful here. If you check this box, it means that you are filing a joint return. If your divorce is final (and you have not remarried), you cannot check this box. If your divorce is not final, you should not check this box if you want to file separately (which we emphatically urge).

We show in Figure 11.1 the first two exemption checkboxes: ☐ Yourself, ☐ Spouse.

We also show several spaces for listing all persons who are your dependents: children and nonchildren. The columnar spaces are for entering (a) full name (first, initial, and last), (b) social security number, (c) relationship, and (d) special $500 credit for each child under age 17. You must enter the social security number of every person you claim as a dependent. If no SSN is entered, or if an incorrect SSN is entered, no exemption is allowed.

Also note in Figure 11.1 that there are two categories of dependent children: custodial and noncustodial. Custodial children are those who live with you (more than six months of the year), whereas noncustodial children are those who do not live with you due to divorce or separation. In the checkboxes to the right, you must designate the distinction. A dependent child, recall, is one for whom you provide more than 50% of his/her total support.

Form 1040	DEPENDENCY EXEMPTIONS			Year

☐ yourself ☐ spouse ← (only if joint return)   Number Caimed → ☐

DEPENDENTS

Name	Soc. Sec. No.	Relation	Credit	
				Custodial Children → ☐
				Noncustodial Children → ☐
				Other Dependents → ☐
		Total Claimed ▶		☐

Fig. 11.1 - Claiming Dependent Children on Form 1040

If a child is not your dependent, even though he/she lived with you, you do *not* use the Figure 11.1 spaces at all. Instead, the child's name (and social security number) is entered at the filing-status checkbox for "Head of household (with qualifying person)."

Evidence of Alimony Paid

If you are a payer of alimony, and you claim a deduction for more than $15,000 in a given year, hard evidence of payment will become an issue. A deduction on Form 1040 of this amount is sizable. The computer is bound to notice it and "red flag" your return . . . for further review.

As we discussed in Chapter 7 (Alimony Payments), stringent tax rules apply. In essence, three particular requirements must be met. One, the payments must be in *cash*. Two, they must be made by an *individual*. Three, they must be an obligation imposed by a state court. Any IRS auditor is going to grill you on at least these three aspects . . . and probably others.

The first thing you will be asked to produce is the court order describing your alimony obligation. It had better be specific. It had better say that you are directed to pay X-dollars per month (per quarter or per year) for alimony (or spousal support). It had better not be clouded with inferences of child support or property settlement. If there is *any inferred wording* of other than pure alimony, all of your payments as deductions will be disallowed.

If you pass the alimony document test, your next hurdle is to produce evidence of payment. Your absolutely best evidence is a batch of monthly canceled checks. Ideally, you would have 12 of such checks arranged in chronological order. If you have, just hand the packet to the auditor. Stay quiet; let the auditor examine every check, one by one, front and back.

The auditor will look for eight features *on each* of the 12 checks. He will look at the name of the payee (1). It had better be your former spouse, as named in the court order (2). He will look to see if the check is drawn on your personal (nonbusiness) account (3). He may even write down on his audit worksheet your checking account number (and may even phone your account holder on the spot) to verify your personal source of payment. He will look at the date of the check (for the year under audit) (4). He will even look for the check being identified as "for alimony" (or spousal support) (5). He will look for your personal handwritten signature (6). He will then flip the check over to see if it is endorsed in the handwriting of the payee, or if it is stamp-endorsed for deposit (7). He will note the date of cancellation and verify if it is the same as the year under audit (8).

Only after he has done these eight examination steps will he add up the total payments for the year. He will then compare these total alimony payments with the total for the preceding year *and* with the total for the following year. If there is a year-to-year increase or decrease by more than $15,000, the excess over $15,000 will be deemed to be for nonalimony obligations.

Evidence of Alimony Received

It is not uncommon for an aggressive payer (usually the ex-husband) to claim an alimony deduction in excess of that which he is court-ordered to pay. He seeks to include child support and/or property settlement payments. He does so with the intent of duping the IRS and intimidating the payee (usually the ex-wife). He wants to shift any IRS audit burden onto the payee.

Suppose, for example, that the payee can extract from all of the divorce papers a reasonably clear paragraph that orders the payer to pay $3,000 per month alimony. Instead, he sends a monthly check for $7,500 to the payee. He memo-marks the check: "For Alimony." In this situation, what does the payee do? Does she report on her Form 1040 $90,000 ($7,500/mo x 12 mo) as "Alimony received"? Or, does she report the receipted amount as $36,000 ($3,000/mo x 12 mo)?

Answer: She reports $36,000 as "Alimony received." Before so, she lays the groundwork for tangling with the payer . . . and with the IRS. Prepare for lots of static and haranguing by the payer and/or by his/her attorney.

As each $7,500 monthly check comes in, the payee first photocopies the check as is. Next, she covers over the memo space (lower left-hand corner) in which the payer has entered "For Alimony." She does so with a self-adhesive correction label. On the correction label affixed to the original check, she makes such notations as (for example):

    ☐ Alimony $3,000   }
    ☐ Child support $2,000   } $7,500
    ☐ Property settlement $2,500 }

She then re-photocopies the check with its memo-corrected notations. After keeping copies of both the original check **and** the correction-notations check, she endorses the check: "For deposit only." She deposits this check separately from all other checks for deposit on the same day.

Next, the payee prepares a "form letter" addressed to the payer. She recites therein the court order (date, page, paragraph) and its specified alimony amount. She acknowledges receipt of the correct amount. She then cites (as below) IRC Section 71(f)(1) re *Excess Alimony Payments*. The two paragraphs of this section read—

(1) If there are excess alimony payments—

*(A) the payer spouse **shall include** the amount of such excess payments **in gross income** for the payer's taxable year . . .*
*(B) the payee spouse **shall be allowed a deduction** in computing adjusted gross income for the amount of such excess payments for the payee's taxable year . . .*
[Emphasis added.]

For each month that the payer sends a check in excess of the correct alimony amount, send to the payer a dated and signed copy of the above form letter. Do not attempt to get him to change his ways. He is playing games with the tax system. Let the IRS induce him to change his ways.

In the described situation, the IRS will first communicate with the payee. Its computer will have picked up a payer-payee mismatching of alimony amounts paid and received. [Recall Figure 7.1 on page 7-5.] To the payee, the IRS will send a *Notice of Proposed Adjustment to Tax Return*. The proposed adjustment (for the example above) would be a $54,000 **addition** ($90,000 – $36,000) to the payee's taxable income. Opportunity will be given to agree, disagree, and/or to explain.

The payee responds to the IRS by sending photocopies of the payer's corrected checks. She also includes a copy of the court order designating the amount of alimony, and a copy of one of her "form letters" that she sent to the payer. Specifically request the IRS to enforce Section 71(f)(1) cited in the form letter. Thereafter, our bet is that the IRS will communicate with the payer with a notice of proposed adjustment.

To summarize the above, we present Figure 11.2. We do so because it is the payee spouse who has to take the initiative when being bulldozed by a payer spouse seeking more tax deductions than those to which he is entitled.

"Split Sale" of Residence

In divorce situations where minor children are involved, family courts often require that the marital residence be occupancy retained by the custodial parent. As such, the court may preclude its sale

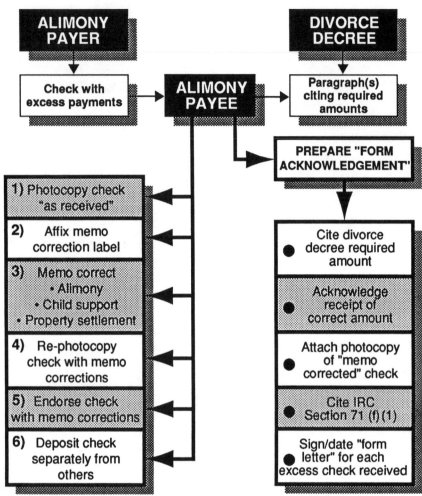

Fig. 11.2 - Procedure by Payee for Correcting "Excess Alimony" by Payer

until one or more minors reach legal age, or until some other financial necessity demands. In these situations, the residence itself becomes the "equalizer" in the final property settlement between the spouses and parents. For property equalizing purposes, for example, Spouse A (the move-out) may be awarded 28% of the sales proceeds. Correspondingly, Spouse B (the stay-in) may be awarded 78% of the sales proceeds [28% + 72% = 100%]. The minute the court decrees a split ownership of the residence, it should be immediately retitled as: *tenants in common*. This protects the ownership interests of the former spouses (who are no longer husband and wife) when the residence is eventually sold.

When real estate is sold, the gross proceeds are reported to the IRS by the closing broker [Sec. 6045(e)]. The electronic form for doing so is Form 1099-S: *Proceeds from Real Estate Transactions*. A hard copy of this form is forwarded to the seller of the property. Unfortunately, the seller's copy is mixed in with a lot of other papers and forms which accompany the sale of any piece of real estate. The result is that Form 1099-S is rarely ever identified and selectively separated out as an important stand-alone tax document.

If the residence is titled in the name of the former husband and former wife, and if there are no instructions to the contrary, Form 1099-S is made out in the former husband's social security number only. He winds up being responsible for **all** of the tax accounting on the sale, even though he may be the judicially mandated "move-out" spouse. This can cause a gross inequity in the transaction.

The way to correct such an inequity is to instruct the real estate reporting broker to issue **two** 1099-Ss. One 1099-S is prepared in the name and SSN of the former husband (showing his percentage of the gross proceeds); the second 1099-S is prepared in the name and SSN of the former wife (showing her percentage of the gross proceeds). For post-sale backup, prepare a "gross proceeds sharing agareement" for signature by each spouse.

Using the 28% and 72% ownership percentages selected for example purposes above, suppose the gross selling price of the former marital residence was $800,000. How would the tenants-in-common sellers instruct the reporting broker?

Answer: Spouse A (the 28% owner) would instruct the real estate broker to report as gross proceeds the amount of $224,000 ($800,000 x 28%). Correspondingly, Spouse B (the 72% owner) would instruct the real estate broker to report as gross proceeds the amount of $576,000 ($800,000 x 72%). Since separate Form 1040 tax returns would be filed, each former spouse is on his or her own. We depict the proper tax reporting in Figure 11.3.

The effect of Figure 11.3 is that of two sales: a 28% sale by Spouse A and a 72% sale by Spouse B. By proportioning only the

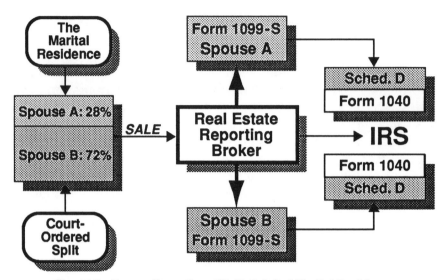

Fig. 11.3 - Proper Reporting: "Split Sale" of Marital Residence

selling price (gross proceeds), the real estate reporting person need only prepare one closing escrow.

Reporting on Schedule D (1040)

Note in Figure 11.3 that we show a Schedule D (Form 1040) emanating from Spouse A's return, and the another separate Schedule D emanating from Spouse B's return. Said Schedule D is titled: *Capital Gains and Losses*. Using the columnized captions on Schedule D, the gain or loss for each former spouse is determined from—

Sales price — Cost or other basis.

Assume that the sales price is $800,000 as above and that the cost or other basis is $300,000. Let us further assume that the move-out Spouse A did so more than three years prior to date of sale. How is the split sale reported on each former spouse's Schedule D (1040)?

Caution: Be aware of Section 121(a) and (b): *Exclusion of Gain from Sale of Principal Residence*. There is a $250,000 capital gain exclusion for each owner who lived in the residence for more than two years in a five-year period ending on date of sale. Thus, Spouse A who moved out more than three years ago does not qualify for the $250,000 exclusion. Spouse B, however, would qualify.

Now, answering the above question, each former spouse would report the sale on his and her Schedule D (1040) as follows:

A's gain $= (800,000 - 300,000) \times 28\%$
$= 500,000 \times 28\% = \$140,000$ **taxable**

B's gain $= (800,000 - 300,000) \times 72\% - \$250,000$ exclusion
$= (500,000 \times 72\%) - 250,000$
$= 360,000 - 250,000 = \$110,000$ **taxable**

From the example above, the move-out spouse has been obviously tax disadvantaged. By being out of his former residence for more than three years, he loses altogether his $250,000 personal residence exclusion. Had he moved out *less than* three years before the sale, his taxable gain would have been "zero" ($140,000 gain − $250,000 exclusion: cannot be less than zero).

There is a strong post-divorce message here. If the move-out spouse anticipates that he would be absent from his former home for three years or more, he should try to get the stay-in spouse to "buy him out." This could be achieved readily with a 2nd trust deed for $140,000 secured on the home (just before sale closing). The stay-in spouse would then own the residence 100%.

In this case, with Section 1041(a) in mind and mentioned in the divorce decree, the move-out spouse would receive his $140,000 at time of sale. Not being a 28% owner any more, he would not have to attach Schedule D to his Form 1040. His $140,000 would then be tax free . . . as "incident to divorce."

Treatment of Rental Property

Unlike a personal residence, there is no $250,000 per owner capital gain exclusion when rental property is sold. Many marital estates consist of one or more parcels of such property: residential and nonresidential. Being real estate, such property produces useful income, has appreciation potential (as an investment), and offers tax sheltering (via depreciation allowances) to modest-income taxpayers. Consequently, unless there is a dire need for post-divorce cash, it is advisable not to sell such property. Instead, the property should be retitled as tenants in common, as per the equity percentages agreed to in the property settlement portion of the decree. This way, each ex-spouse continues as a co-owner of a valuable investment item.

Rental property is a natural target for IRS audit, irrespective of divorce. This is because most property owners want to accelerate all the depreciation they can. This gives them some tax shelter. In addition, there are numerous expenses which are tax deductible, such as travel, repairs, supplies, utilities, insurance, mortgage interest, and so on. These, too, provide some tax shelter. The IRS has an aversion to all forms of tax shelters, so it goes on the attack. Divorce provides the audit opportunity that the IRS is looking for.

Many spouses after divorce continue communicating with each other on tax and fiscal affairs. Often, they agree to continue co-owning their rental property in such a way that the lower-income party gets most of the rental income, and the higher-income party gets most of the tax deductions. For example, a 15% tax-rate spouse would pay less tax on (say) $9,000 of rental income than would a 30% tax-rate spouse. Conversely, some $9,000 worth of deductions (depreciation and expenses) would be more tax beneficial to the 30% tax-rate spouse than to the 15% spouse. Not being husband and wife anymore, these kinds of post-divorce arrangements are legal, but are subject to tax scrutiny. Therefore, be forewarned. Formalize the arrangement by retitling the property.

An auditor's first step in the scrutinizing process is to request the *title deed* (along with the divorce decree). If the title is still in the name of the parties as husband and wife, he has found pay dirt. "The title is defective," he'll blurt. Then abruptly he will disallow all deductions and assign all income to the higher-income party. He is instructed to do this, to pull in the maximum revenue.

Suppose the title is in joint tenancy as unmarried man and unmarried woman. And suppose they agree that the man would get 70% of the deductions, whereas the woman would get 70% of the income. What then?

The auditor would ask to see a written partnership agreement between the two unrelated parties. Said agreement should spell out each party's share of ownership, income, depreciation, expenses, and management of the property. If there is no such agreement in writing, the auditor arbitrarily cuts everything down the middle, 50/50. If the title were tenants in common (non 50/50) instead of joint tenancy, the auditor would assign the income and deductions in accordance with the specified ownership percentages of each party.

If there is a notarized written agreement between the co-owners, the parties can shift the income and deductions between each other as they like. As an example of what can be done, we present Figure 11.4. We are using the simple numbers discussed above so that you can get the idea. Be aware that the *allocation* of income and deductions applies while the property is being held for rent. When it is sold, the equity, basis, and capital gain portions are the specified portions in the title deed.

RENTAL INCOME PROPERTY
Co-Owned with "Allocation Agreement"

ITEM	Former Spouse A	Former Spouse B
Tax Bracket	30%	15%
Agreement Terms		
• Income	30%	70%
• Deductions	70%	30%
Amount if $9,000		
• Income	$2,700	$6,300
• Deductions	$6,300	$2,700
Net Income/Loss	(3,600)	3,600
Income Tax	(1,080) *	540
Spendable After Tax	1,080	3,060

*This is the amount of tax reduced on other sources of income.

Fig. 11.4 - Shifting After-Divorce Income with Rental Property

As indicated in Figure 11.4, the higher tax bracket former spouse has a tax recognized loss of <$3,600>. This saves him $1,080 [<$3,600> x 30%] in taxes elsewhere on his return.

Although the lower tax bracket former spouse has a positive income of $3,600, she pays only $540 tax ($3,600 x 15%) on that amount. As illustrated, both former spouses have spendable income after tax. Our point is that both former spouses can continue to benefit from rental property after the divorce. Do things right and keep good co-ownership records.

Notify Banks, Brokers, Payers, Etc.

In addition to the residence (and possibly other real estate), marital property often consists of accounts with banks, brokerage firms, mutual funds, insurance companies, pension plans, and other custodial accounts (trusts, estates, partnerships). When these accounts are rearranged into separate portions for each former spouse, it is incumbent that the custodians be notified of all changes: names, addresses, social security numbers, amounts retained, amounts transferred, etc. As you know, each custodian reports to the IRS electronically on such forms as 1099-INT (for interest paid), 1099-DIV (for dividends paid), 1099-B (for securities sales), 1099-R (for retirement distributions), and K-1s (for trusts, estates, and partnerships). Collectively, the activities are called: "broker reportings."

In post-divorce situations, can you not imagine the utter confusion that can result from these broker reportings? Different ownership percentages and different accounts going back and forth between former spouses with different social security numbers . . . what a reporting mess!

Suppose, for example, a husband (the transferor) assigns 20,000 shares of the XYZ mutual fund to his wife (the transferee). The per share value at the time is $3.50. He gives the broker his wife's name, address, and social security number. A few months later, in the same tax year through the same broker, the wife sells the 20,000 shares at the then value of $4.25 per share. What is the broker likely to report to the IRS?

Answer: He is likely to issue *two* Forms 1099-B: *Proceeds from Broker and Barter Transaction.* One would be issued in the name (and social security number) of the husband, showing redemption proceeds of $70,000 (20,000 shares at $3.50 per share).

A second 1099-B would be issued in the name (and social security number) of the wife, showing sale proceeds of $85,000 (20,000 shares at $4.25 per share). By so doing, the IRS and its computer are looking to tax *both* the $70,000 and the $85,000 reportings. In actuality, only the $85,000 sale is a taxable transaction.

More correctly, the broker, when debiting the husband's account should indicate the 20,000 shares as being a nontaxable transaction under the provisions of Section 1041(a). This way, only the wife need be issued a 1099-B. When the IRS "sees" the wife's $85,000 sale, it will computer search her Form 1040 (with Schedule D attached) to assure that the $85,000 is reported and that the gain or loss is properly computed.

Trusts, Partnerships, & S Corporations

Many marital estates consist of income and distributions from family trusts, limited partnerships, and S corporations. These distributions are reported to the IRS via information returns called: "K-1s" (Schedules K-1, that is). The K-1s are titled: [Recipient's] *Share of Income, Credits, Deductions, etc.* There is a K-1 (Form 1041) for trusts; a K-1 (Form 1065) for partnerships; and a K-1 (Form 1120S) for S corporations. For trusts, the K-1 recipient is a *Beneficiary*; for partnerships, the recipient is a *Partner*; for S corporations, the recipient is a *Shareholder.*

During marriage, a recipient's reporting of the K-1 information on Form 1040 for computer cross-matching by the IRS is confusing and irritating. After divorce, the computer-matching situation worsens by far. As a result, the property settlement issues on K-1 matters are often silent. It is better to resolve these matters with a Divorce Modification Order before the IRS gets in the act.

In the case of distributions from a family trust, post-divorce resolution can be rather simple. This is because the origin of trust property derives from the trustor (creator) of the trust. If the trustor is a parent or blood relative of the husband, the distributions from the trust are his separate property. Similarly for trust distributions where the trustor is a parent or blood relative of the wife. Other than notifying the trustee of each trust of any applicable change of address, the K-1 to a distributee is unaffected.

Post-divorce distributions from a limited partnership or an S corporation are a different (more complicated) matter. These are passive investment entities where tax sheltering (via special credits and deductions) comprises their principal benefit. While married, the capital contributions to these entities often are in increments of $5,000 . . . to perhaps around $20,000. Over a few years' time, the cash value in each entity dwindles to under $1,000. Trying to clarify which spouse gets possession of each limited partnership or each S corporation can cost more in legal fees than the cash worth of all entities combined. Here's where the "coin toss" approach is the best course of property settlement. Simply toss a coin, call it, and assign all residual worth to one spouse only.

Why do we suggest doing this?

Because the K-1s issued by each entity for each ongoing post-divorce year will drive the coin toss transferee wild. Better there be one such transferee than two. The one transferee can pursue his/her own judgmental actions for closing out the K-1 irritations.

For each K-1, there can be from three to 10 items of tax information computer matched by the IRS. Whether an item is $5 positive or $18 negative in amount, the IRS makes no common sense judgment call whatsoever. To its computer, a $5 reportable item is process treated exactly the same way as though it were a $50,000 item. If there is no corresponding Form 1040 reporting of each $3, $20, or <$16> K-1 item reported, a harrowing experience of computer-matching tyranny (by the IRS) springs forth.

Just because your decree of divorce is final, it does not mean that you are out of the tax forest. There are many followup tax matters that can come out of the woodwork. Simpy be aware . . . and be prepared. Your tax life goes on long after your divorce experience fades.

12

REMARITAL ASPECTS

Sooner Or Later, Most Divorced Persons Do Remarry. In The Preparatory Stages, Many New Tax Precautions Are Required. These Include Scrupulously Separate Tax Records During Any Period Of "Singles Together." When Remarriage Is Set, A Written "Prenuptial Agreement" Is Urged. The Idea Is To Keep Separate Property Trails — And File Separate Tax Returns — For 3 To 5 Years Into The New Marriage. Several "Bad Examples" Are Cited Which Highlight The Consequences Of Too-Hasty Commingling. If Remarriage Occurs, Prudence Suggests A Well-Thought-Through (3 To 5 Years) Deferred Commingling "Plan."

Divorce is not the end of your world. Yes, there are emotional, family, occupational, financial, and tax strains involved. These strains also can be brought on by other events in one's life. They can cause temporary setbacks. Nevertheless, life after divorce must go on. In the process, seek to do better.

Once the legal aspects of divorce have cleared, many persons begin rethinking their lives in terms of remarriage. This is not something that everyone rushes into. Yet, the possibility does cross one's mind. It is a fact that more divorced persons remarry than those who do not remarry.

If there is any chance of your remarriage, we want you to know that there are tax pitfalls ahead. Pitfalls exist becaue you now have a *trail* of tax ramifications which you never had at the time of your first marriage. There are many aspects of your divorce settlement which will linger for a long time. Consequently your tax affairs — at least for the next several years — will be more complicated than any of your prior experiences. So, do proceed with tax caution.

The Prelude: Singles Together

Following a divorce, many persons take on cohabitational living with another person of the opposite sex. Among the reasons for doing so are the need for emotional readjustment, financial accommodation, companionship, and — perhaps — the expectation of remarriage. This is what we call "singles together." The arrangement creates a tax lifestyle all of its own.

Man and woman living together is basic to human nature. If they do so as husband wife, their tax affairs are simplified through a joint return. If they live together not as husband and wife, their tax affairs are quite different from two singles who are not living together. Many property holdings and living expenses are shared. This leads to certain tax temptations in a joint effort to reduce their combined tax take by the IRS.

The common living together situation is that one person owns or rents a personal residence, and the other person simply moves in. There is invitation, followed by mutual consent and agreement.

Once the other person moves in, many of the household living expenses are shared. Quite often, the sharing is unequal on a dollar-for-dollar basis. Typically, one person pays more than 50% of the total support and maintenance of the other. In every ordinary respect, the move-in person becomes a member of the taxpayer's household.

Thus, the first tax question arises: Can the move-in person be claimed as a dependent on the taxpayer's return?

The answer is "Yes" . . . *under certain conditions*. But keep in mind that the move-in person is not an ordinary family member.

The first requirement of any dependency claim is the amount of total support for the dependent. If the taxpayer pays more than 50% of the move-in person's total support (food, shelter, etc.), then one of the dependency tests is met.

A second requirement is that the move-in must have no taxable income requiring the filing of her (or his) own tax return. Here, the term "taxable" excludes child support payments and other nontaxable income that the move-in may receive from others.

The next requirement is a "full taxable year." This is set forth in Section 152(a)(9) to wit:

The term "dependent" means . . . an individual (other than an individual who at any time during the taxable year was the spouse . . . of the taxpayer) who, for the taxable year of the taxpayer, has as his principal place of abode the home of the taxpayer and is a member of the taxpayer's household.

What this says is that if one is divorced at any time during a given year, and has a move-in during or prior to the divorce year, there is no way that the move-in can be claimed as a dependent. Section 152(a)(9) upholds the legal premise of marriage. That is, one legally has a spouse, whether living with such spouse or not, up until the final decree. It is not until the first full year after divorce that a move-in can be claimed as a dependent (if the support test is met). In other words, there must be a full 12 months' residency, January through December, to qualify as a member-of-household dependent. Note the phrase above: "for the taxable year."

For move-ins, the all-important dependency test is nonviolation of local law. This is covered by Section 152(b)(5) which reads—

An individual is not a member of the taxpayer's household if at any time during the taxable year . . . the relationship between such individual and the taxpayer is in violation of local law.

If there is no local law or ordinance against the voluntary cohabitation of man and woman, then a move-in may indeed be claimed as a dependent. Even if there is such a law, but it is not regularly enforced, the move-in can still be claimed as a dependent.

If the conditions above are met, the taxpayer is entitled to one dependency exemption for the move-in person. However, he has to show the name of the dependent, that person's social security number, the relationship (member of household) and the number of months of residency (must be 12). Said exemption is not as tax advantageous as if the move-in were the taxpayer's spouse.

Joint Returns Spell Trouble

Man and woman living together in a lifestyle as though husband and wife begin to think of each other as spouses. They live and act as such. The only difference is that they have not formalized their relationship in a marriage ceremony with a certificate. Often, such singles together consider their arrangement a "common law" marriage. So, what happens if they file a joint return together?

The answer: Maybe nothing, but also . . . maybe trouble. Various tax penalties could be imposed.

In this day and age, it is not uncommon for a husband and wife (legally married) to file a joint return keeping their names separate. Instead of a common last name (the husband's), two full names are used, such as

John J. Jones & Mary M. Martin

Today, it is not even a requirement that the husband's name go first on a tax return. For married taxpayers, the order could be

Mary M. Martin & John J. Jones

The IRS will accept such returns, so long as the social security number of each spouse is appropriately entered on Form 1040. That is, if the husband's name is first, his social security number must be listed first. If the wife's name is first, her social security number must be listed first.

With this joint filing procedure now recognized as acceptably proper, what would happen if two singles living together did the same thing?

If the singles got married shortly after filing a joint return, chances are their filing would never be picked up in the normal screening process. But if marriage did not take place within a reasonable length of time (after filing a joint return as unmarrieds), the singles are taking gambler risks. They are gambling against the Computer.

If both singles are divorced, they would be very foolish to file a joint return before remarriage. Surprisingly, certain "signals of divorce" flash through. For example, if the taxpayer is paying alimony, and claims it as a deduction on the joint return, some suspicions might arise. A real telltale signal develops where the move-in person receives alimony and reports same on the joint return. Recall Figure 7.1 on page 7-5.

Can't you imagine the IRS's computer "red-alert" flashings when it sees a joint return with alimony received and alimony paid on the *same* return? (Again, Figure 7.1.) Although this is possible for a bona fide divorce (from one spouse) and a bona fide remarriage (to a different spouse) within the same year, it is, nevertheless, a suspicious "double entry." If addresses and social security numbers on prior returns conflict with the current return in any way, an improper filing is assumed.

Another way that an improper joint return could be picked up is by a report to the IRS by a former spouse. Embittered former spouses have a way of keeping track of their move-out spouses for violations of law. If they suspect a joint return improperly filed, and are seeking revenge in some way, they could report the two singles to the IRS.

Still another way is a complaint to the IRS by the move-in person. When two singles file a joint return, there is an implication that marriage is in the offing. Should the move-in become fearful that marriage is not in prospect, there is likelihood of complaint that the joint return was filed fraudulently and under duress. This almost certainly would provoke an audit and a redetermination of the tax based on two separate returns. A joint return can only be filed by married individuals, and by no others.

Filing Status Options

Two singles living together without children have just two filing options. They can file one return: taxpayer (single status) plus one dependent (the move-in). Or, they can file two separate returns: each as a single status. But if one or more children are in the singles household, creative options open up.

Consider, for example, that the taxpayer has no children but the move-in has one child. The move-in receives a small amount of alimony and child support, but otherwise does not work. The taxpayer pays more than 50% of the total support for the child in his household. What arrangements can the taxpayer and move-in make as to their own filing status?

The taxpayer can file single with one dependent (the move-in's child). The move-in can qualify on her own separate return as head of household. The child would be listed as the qualifying person of the move-in, but not as a dependent. The move-in can justify head of household status on the grounds that her alimony plus "contributions" by the taxpayer are used to pay more than 50% of the household support of her child. The taxpayer cannot claim head of household status because it is not his child.

Let's consider another case. The taxpayer has one dependent child in the singles household and the move-in also has one child. The move-in receives a small amount of alimony and child support, as above. How can they now file?

Each can file as head of household with one dependent. The taxpayer and his child; the move-in and her child. Where the move-in's support for her child is less than the amount of child support that she receives, she arranges with the taxpayer to make contributions for her child's support. If her contributions together with the taxpayer's contributions exceed 50% of the child's total support, she can claim her child as a dependent.

Importance of Prenuptial Agreement

Sooner or later, most singles living together do marry. They may not always marry each other. More often, they split up and marry other singles who are divorced or widowed. Fully 85% of all those who are divorced or widowed below age 60 do remarry.

Upon agreement to marriage and the setting of the second (or third) wedding date, there are many tax, financial, and property matters to be worked out. It is necessary to do this so that there is clear understanding of each partner's position after the marriage ceremony. The time to do this is *before* the wedding and thereby before any post-wedding problems develop. The manner of doing so is via a *prenuptial agreement* . . . in written form.

Why is a prenuptial agreement so important? Why can't the parties just get married and start living the new life that they want?

If any post-marital problems develop, why can't they work out an agreement at the time? Won't any written instrument before marriage only create doubts and suspicions about the seriousness of the marriage?

Rather than trying to answer each of these and other questions, let us cite a common example of why a prenuptial agreement can be important. We will cite from an actual case history, with editorial variations to avoid identity of the parties involved.

The husband-to-be was a wheeler-dealer in a not-too-successful business. He was involved in various lawsuits; had run-ins with tax authorities; and was just plan inattentive to financial recordkeeping. But he was a charmer and a ladies' man: much sought after in marriage. The wife-to-be was convinced that he had changed his ways and that things would be different in their marriage. She was a working woman making good income. She poo-poohed any suggestion that she prepare a prenuptial agreement.

The wedding took place as scheduled. At the end of the year, they filed a joint 1040 tax return. The return showed a $2,215 refund, due mostly to the wife's withholdings.

Subsequent to filing the return, but before the refund came, the wife stumbled onto some of the husband's tax records. She came across a form with the heading: FINAL NOTICE BEFORE SEIZURE. It was an IRS demand for $27,629 including penalties and interest. When she confronted her husband with the form, he responded triumphantly: "It's all been taken care of. You see, it's dated more than three years ago. There has been no correspondence since. I assure you, sweetheart, you have nothing to worry about."

A few weeks later, a notice was received from the IRS that the $2,215 "refund" was credited against the $27,629 delinquency. The balance due was $25,414 . . . plus further penalties and interest until paid in full.

Just because one "hears nothing" from the IRS does not mean that a tax matter is closed. The IRS has up to ten years after assessment of tax to start collection thereon. As long as it *starts* collection, the collection process can go on indefinitely.

In the case cited above, collection began with the $2,215 credit of the "refund" against the $27,629 delinquency. The credit notice took place within the statutory ten years of the date of the seizure notice. As long as a joint return is filed, collection will continue against the wife. The situation could have been avoided by a "hold harmless" tax clause in a written prenuptial agreement.

Sample Prenuptial Wording

The written agreement need not be any formal or fancy legal document. It need not even be prepared by an attorney. It can be prepared by the spouses themselves, or by others in the professional world. Of course, if the affairs of one party are truly complicated, such as where considerable wealth or an intricate family business is involved, a competent contract attorney should be sought. Otherwise, a simple personal contract between the spouses-to-be is all that is needed.

In format, the contract consists of four elements. These are: (a) preamble, (b) reference facts, (c) agreement paragraphs, and (d) signatures and notarization. For proper identity, the contract should be labeled: PRENUPTIAL AGREEMENT. A copy should be kept with each party's important papers.

The preamble is a short introductory statement which identifies the parties involved and the scope of the coverage. This introductory statement should read along the following lines:

THIS AGREEMENT *is made by and between* JOHN J. JONES *hereinafter referred to as "Husband" and* MARY M. MARTIN *hereinafter referred to as "Wife." It is made prior to their marriage with reference to the financial and property affairs after marriage.*

It is next necessary to cite certain background facts so that the "important cards" are on the table. The idea is that there be adequate disclosure between the parties, to avoid any implication of threats or duress. They are verifiable reference facts on which each party relies. They should be enumerated in 1-2-3 fashion along the lines presented in Figure 12.1.

With the reference facts on record, the specific terms of agreement are then set forth. The "agreement" is actually a series of subagreements. Each subagreement is a separate subject addressed

PRENUPTIAL AGREEMENT

PREAMBLE (as in the text)

THE FACTS upon which this agreement is made are as follows:

1. The parties have agreed to become married on or about ___(date)___ .

2. The Husband was previously married for approximately _____ years, and was divorced on ___(date)___ .

3. The Wife was previously married for approximately _____ years, and is a widow. Her previous husband deceased on ___(date)___ .

4. The Husband has two children, namely: DONALD D. JONES, born __(date)__ , and OLIVIA O. JONES, born __(date)__ .

5. The Wife has one child, namely : CHRISTOPHER C. MARTIN, born __(date)__ .

6. The Husband has that property interest enumerated and valued in Exibit A.

7. The Wife has that property interest enumerated and valued in Exibit B.

8. All known debts and liabilities of both Husband and Wife are identified by source and amount in Exhibit C. Included therein are alimony and child support payments to be made by the Husband.

9. The Husband is employed by ____(company)____ ; the Wife is not employed.

NOW, THEREFORE, IT IS MUTUALLY AGREED THAT -

ITEMIZED SUBAGREEMENTS

IN WITNESS WHEREOF this instrument is executed this _____(date)_____ at _____(city)_____ , _____(state)_____ .

/s/
_____
John J. Jones, Husband

/s/
_____
Mary M. Martin, Wife

(Verification and Seal of Notary Public)

Fig. 12.1 - Sample Format of Prenuptial Agreement

in a separate paragraph of its own. This is so that if one subject is subsequently amended or terminated, the remaining subagreements are still contractually valid. Each subject carries a short, identifying, lead-in caption, such as—

    a. Support or children
    b. Warranty against prior liabilities
    c. Prior income tax returns
    d. Property warranty
    e. Separate property interests
    f. Separate property records
    g. Beneficiaries of insurance, pensions, etc.
    h. Marital property estate

Once the agreement paragraphs have been written and reviewed, the concluding effort is the signatures of both parties in the presence of each other. Although not absolutely essential, it is good practice to have the agreement signed in the presence of a Notary Public. This adds the weight of a non-interested third party as an official witness.

Case of Imprudent Commingling

Commingling is the process whereby two parties with a common interest mix and interchange their separate assets in such a way that the separate character can no longer be identified. Whether intended to be so or not, the "mixture" becomes cotenancy property. The dictionary definition of *commingle* is: "to blend thoroughly into an harmonious whole; to combine (funds or property) into a common entity."

Two persons, man and woman, getting remarried do indeed consider themselves to be a common entity. Such an arrangement is the basic unit of civilized societies. But there are — or can be — pitfalls and problems with remarital commingling. There can be tax problems, financial problems, legal problems, estate problems, and other just plain accounting problems. Prudent parties remarrying should take precautions against these problems. A real-life case on point follows.

After 15 years of marriage, Taxpayer H got divorced. About six months later, he married Taxpayer W who had been twice divorced. Taxpayer H was self-employed and netted about $35,000 per year from his business. They agreed to convert all of their checking and savings accounts into cotenancy form.

Prior to remarriage, the husband had three bank accounts: personal checking, business checking, and personal savings. The wife had two accounts: personal checking and personal savings. Upon remarriage, the husband closed out his former accounts and opened up three new accounts: joint checking, business checking, and joint savings. Approximately $31,000 was involved in the opening balances of these new accounts. The wife did not close either of her accounts, claiming that she had less than $100 in each.

The marriage lasted exactly three months and ten days. During this time, the husband had deposited $19,000 (approximately) in his new business account. The attorney for the wife demanded $25,000 for settlement. This was "one-half," he said, of the $31,000 plus $19,000 (total $50,000) marital estate.

The husband replied: "That's ridiculous. I'll take it to my tax accountant; he'll know what to do."

The accountant, having had experience with *bank deposits analysis* in IRS audits of self-employed persons, knew exactly what to do. He obtained, through the husband's attorney, photocopies of all bank statements one month preceding the date of marriage, bank statements for each month of marriage, and bank statements for one month following the date of separation. He was able to trace, entry by entry, the amounts that were the husband's separate property before marriage. With corresponding annotation on the old and new accounts, he identified approximately $29,000 as being clearly the husband's. This left a potential marital estate of $21,000 ($50,000 minus $29,000).

During the three months of marriage, there was a total of approximately $16,000 debited against the three joint accounts. The attorney for the wife conveniently forgot to mention this $16,000 of marital debts. So, altogether, the net marital estate was $5,000 ($21,000 minus $16,000). Of this, the wife was entitled to one-half, or $2,500: NOT the $25,000 initially demanded.

As to the wife's two former accounts which were not closed, there were deposits but no debits. During the three months of marriage, a total of $3,000 was deposited. When confronted about this, the wife claimed that it was her money from her wages. The attorney for the husband countered that *half* was her money and half was her husband's. The "one-half" of a marital estate works both ways. In court, the judge approved a $1,000 marital settlement ($2,500 minus $1,500) to the wife. He also approved a $5,000 attorney fee against the husband. The matter dragged on for 18 months before settlement — six times the length of the marriage!

The situation above could have been quite different, had the husband not rushed into commingling all of his bank accounts so promptly. The parties could have set up just **one** joint account: personal checking. They could have opened the account with approximately equal initial amounts. From the date of marriage on, the husband could have deposited the net earnings from his business, and the wife also could have deposited the net wages from her employment. When the marriage broke up, there would have been one account to be analyzed: not the eight above (3 his, 3 joint, 2 hers). Any divorce distribution would have been pure 50/50.

"Theft" of Premarital Residences

Here's another bad example where deferred commingling should have been practiced. This is truly a painful case.

Taxpayer W was married eight years and got divorced. She got an $18,000 cash settlement. She used this money to buy her first residence. About a year later, she sold Residence #1 and made a profit of about $20,000.

With the proceeds of the first sale, she bought Residence #2. A year "plus" later she sold this residence for a cumulative gain of $35,000. She then bought Residence #3 which she held for three years before selling.

While in Residence #3, Taxpayer H (an attorney who was divorced) moved in and lived with Taxpayer W as singles together. Since taxpayer W had no significant income of her own, she allowed H to make mortgage payments on Residence #3. He did this from his separate checking account. As a consequence, H began pressing W to add his name to the title deed of Residence #3. W refused saying: "Not until we get married."

They did get married, but before the husband's name was added to Residence #3, it was sold. At this point, there was a cumulative gain of about $88,000 on all three of W's residences. At the sale closing, the wife allowed her attorney husband to review and sign the escrow papers. The sale closed, whereupon a check for $82,000 net proceeds (gain minus selling expenses) was made payable solely to the wife. The husband took the check, telling the wife that he would hold it as "collateral" until they bought Residence #4 as joint tenants.

After living in Residence #4 for nearly two years, the wife made persistent inquiry to her husband as to the whereabouts of her $82,000 check. He told her: "I cashed it and 'we' bought tax shelters with it." To which the wife countered: "How could you cash that check? It had only my name on it. That was my separate property." The husband smiled saying, "I signed it. I have your tacit power of attorney. I am your husband and I am also your attorney. Besides, the check was community property since it was made out after we were married." (Hogwash!)

From this point on, their marital relations grew worse. The husband moved out of Residence #4 and stopped making the mortgage payments. He also borrowed money against the equity in the house, which became a lien against it. The mortgage holder started foreclosure proceedings, at which point the wife put the house up for sale. It sold for a cumulative gain of $325,000.

The husband claimed that half of this cumulative gain was his. He refused to allow the sale to close unless he was given $162,500 of the proceeds. In desperation, the wife gave in. She needed the money to live on, as her husband had stopped supporting her.

After the sale of Residence #4, the wife filed for divorce. In the meantime, the IRS had disallowed the tax shelters which the husband had bought, and demanded $80,000 in taxes not paid. The husband contended that the wife would have to pay $40,000 of the tax, before he would agree to the divorce. Under duress, she agreed. Later, however, she filed for innocent spouse tax relief.

There is an important lesson to be learned from this case. If one party has a sequence of personal residences before marriage, overt effort must be made to keep the residence(s), and all the records thereon, as one's own separate property. There is no law requiring commingling, even after marriage, where property has a separate character before marriage.

In the situation above, the separate property interests of the wife should have been protected through the sale of Residence #3. The

$82,000 check should have gone into the wife's separate checking/savings account. She should have sought separate legal counsel at that time. Disturbingly enough, the attorney husband never opened a joint bank account with his wife. Proper commingling should have started with Residence #4.

Deferred Commingling Plan

Deferred commingling has much to be said for it. First of all, it is a practical form of postnuptial compliance with a prenuptial agreement, whether written or oral. Secondly, it starts the remarrieds onto a more self-disciplined accounting agreement. And, thirdly, it provides a transitional period for phase-in to full commingling. This transitional effort becomes a period of probational cooperation for getting the new marriage on solid ground. The proper handling of tax and financial matters can go a long way in consolidating a remarriage.

For most effective "getting on solid ground," some form of deferred-commingling *plan* is required. A "plan" means that the parties discuss — and agree — on how they are going to merge (commingle) their affairs, and over what period of time. As a plan, it should be in writing. It does not require the formality of a prenuptial agreement.

A deferred-commingling plan would have little or no legal standing in the event the parties broke up. Its only legal attributes would be the separate accounts maintained up to the point of breakup. If breakup occurs, the fallback document for legal standing is the prenuptial agreement. Hence, a deferred-commingling plan is a supplement to the prenuptial agreement: *not* a substitute for it.

Any agreement called a "plan" should have a starting date and a terminal date. Our recommendation is that the starting date be the day after date of remarriage. The terminal date should be no less than three — and no more than five — full calendar years later. The term "full calendar year" means a 12-month period following December 31 of the year of marriage. This means that unless the wedding takes place on January 1, the year of remarriage will always be less than a full calendar year.

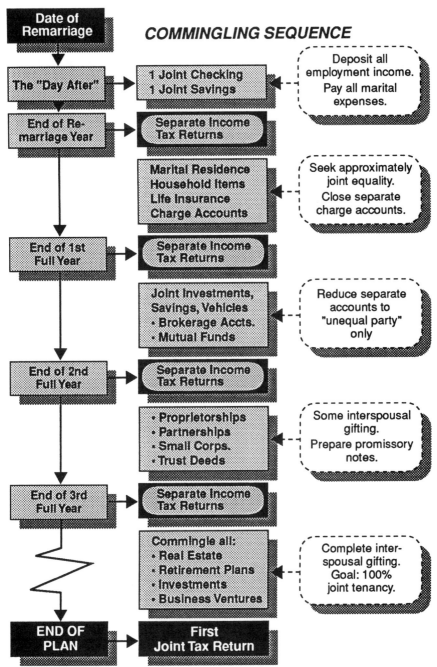

Fig. 12.2 - Outline for a Deferred Commingling "Plan"

The overall intent of the plan should be that, until termination, each party should file a separate tax return on his *and* her own. Thus, at the minimum there would be four years of separate returns (year of marriage plus three) . . . or six years at the maximum. Filing separate tax returns for four to six years in a remarriage lasting 10, 20, 30 or more years is a minor inconvenience for the probational benefits gained.

We present Figure 12.2 as an outline of how a deferred commingling plan might be organized. The commingling is "programmed" in such a way that the major assets prior to the remarriage (real estate, retirement plans, etc.) are deferred until last. Should the marriage not endure, these assets — because of their dollar magnitude — would become primary bones of contention in a divorce settlement. If these assets are maintained as separate property, any disharmony before the end of the plan could be settled without great dollar pain.

The end objective of a deferred commingling plan is to attain 100% commingling. From this point on, all marital assets are co-owned 50/50. There is no more separate property by either spouse. Joint tax returns are filed, and there is joint planning towards retirement . . . and world travel.

ABOUT
THE AUTHOR

Holmes F. Crouch

Born on a small farm in southern Maryland, Holmes was graduated from the U.S. Coast Guard Academy with a Bachelor's Degree in Marine Engineering. While serving on active duty, he wrote many technical articles on maritime matters. After attaining the rank of Lieutenant Commander, he resigned to pursue a career as a nuclear engineer.

Continuing his education, he earned a Master's Degree in Nuclear Engineering from the University of California. He also authored two books on nuclear propulsion. As a result of the tax write-offs associated with writing these books, the IRS audited his returns. The IRS's handling of the audit procedure so annoyed Holmes that he undertook to become as knowledgeable as possible regarding tax procedures. He became a licensed private Tax Practitioner by passing an examination administered by the IRS. Having attained this credential, he started his own tax preparation and counseling business in 1972.

In the early years of his tax practice, he was a regular talk-show guest on San Francisco's KGO Radio responding to hundreds of phone-in tax questions from listeners. He was a much sought-after guest speaker at many business seminars and taxpayer meetings. He also provided counseling on special tax problems, such as divorce matters, property exchanges, timber harvesting, mining ventures, animal breeding, independent contractors, selling businesses, and offices-at-home. Over the past 25 years, he has prepared well over 10,000 tax returns for individuals, estates, trusts, and small businesses (in partnership and corporate form).

During the tax season of January through April, he prepares returns in a unique manner. During a single meeting, he completes the return . . . *on the spot!* The client leaves with his return signed, sealed, and in a stamped envelope. His unique approach to preparing returns and his personal interest in his clients' tax affairs have honed his professional proficiency. His expertise extends through itemized deductions, computer-matching of income sources, capital gains and losses, business expenses and cost of goods, residential rental expenses, limited and general partnership activities, closely-held corporations, to family farms and ranches.

He remembers spending 12 straight hours completing a doctor's complex return. The next year, the doctor, having moved away, utilized a large accounting firm to prepare his return. Their accountant was so impressed by the manner in which the prior return was prepared that he recommended the doctor travel the 500 miles each year to have Holmes continue doing it.

He recalls preparing a return for an unemployed welder, for which he charged no fee. Two years later the welder came back and had his return prepared. He paid the regular fee . . . and then added a $300 tip.

During the off season, he represents clients at IRS audits and appeals. In one case a shoe salesman's audit was scheduled to last three hours. However, after examining Holmes' documentation it was concluded in 15 minutes with "no change" to his return. In another instance he went to an audit of a custom jeweler that the IRS dragged out for more than six hours. But, supported by Holmes' documentation, the client's return was accepted by the IRS with "no change."

Then there was the audit of a language translator that lasted two full days. The auditor scrutinized more than $1.25 million in gross receipts, all direct costs, and operating expenses. Even though all expensed items were documented and verified, the auditor decided that more than $23,000 of expenses ought to be listed as capital items for depreciation instead. If this had been enforced it would have resulted in a significant additional amount of tax. Holmes strongly disagreed and after many hours explanation got the amount reduced by more than 60% on behalf of his client.

He has dealt extensively with gift, death and trust tax returns. These preparations have involved him in the tax aspects of wills, estate planning, trustee duties, probate, marital and charitable bequests, gift and death exemptions, and property titling.

Although not an attorney, he prepares Petitions to the U.S. Tax Court for clients. He details the IRS errors and taxpayer facts by citing pertinent sections of tax law and regulations. In a recent case involving an attorney's ex-spouse, the IRS asserted a tax deficiency of $155,000. On behalf of his client, he petitioned the Tax Court and within six months the IRS conceded the case.

Over the years, Holmes has observed that the IRS is not the industrious, impartial, and competent federal agency that its official public imaging would have us believe.

He found that, at times, under the slightest pretext, the IRS has interpreted against a taxpayer in order to assess maximum penalties, and may even delay pending matters so as to increase interest due on additional taxes. He has confronted the IRS in his own behalf on five separate occasions, going before the U.S. Claims Court, U.S. District Court, and U.S. Tax Court. These were court actions that tested specific sections of the Internal Revenue Code which he found ambiguous, inequitable, and abusively interpreted by the IRS.

Disturbed by the conduct of the IRS and by the general lack of tax knowledge by most individuals, he began an innovative series of taxpayer-oriented Federal tax guides. To fulfill this need, he undertook the writing of a series of guidebooks that provide in-depth knowledge on one tax subject at a time. He focuses on subjects that plague taxpayers all throughout the year. Hence, his formulation of the "Allyear" Tax Guide series.

The author is indebted to his wife, Irma Jean, and daughter, Barbara MacRae, for the word processing and computer graphics that turn his experiences into the reality of these publications. Holmes welcomes comments, questions, and suggestions from his readers. He can be contacted in California at (408) 867-2628, or by writing to the publisher's address.

ALLYEAR Tax Guides
by Holmes F. Crouch

For information about the above titles,
and/or a free 8 page catalog, contact:

www.allyeartax.com

Phone: (408) 867-2628   Fax: (408) 867-6466